The Effective Pastor

The Effective Pastor

A Guide to Successful Ministry

Louis W. Bloede

Fortress Press
Minneapolis

Library of Congress Cataloging-in-Publication Data
Bloede, Louis W.
    The effective pastor : a guide to successful ministry / Louis W. Bloede.
       p. cm.
    Includes bibliographical references.
    ISBN 0-8006-2787-3 (alk. paper)
    1. Pastoral theology.   I. Title.
BV4011.2.B56   1996
253'.2—dc20

96-3869
CIP

The paper used in this publication meets the minimum requirements of American National Standard for Information Sciences—Permanence of Paper for Printed Library Materials, ANSI Z329.48-1984.

Manufactured in the U.S.A.   AF 1-2787
01   00   99   98   97   96   1   2   3   4   5   6   7   8   9   10

Contents

Acknowledgments

Although the cover of this book lists one person as author, any author knows that what one writes includes ideas and information from many sources. Likewise, the preparation of the manuscript for publishing involves the work of a number of persons.

My appreciation extends back to Salem United Methodist Church in Fond du Lac, Wisconsin, the congregation that nurtured me in the Christian faith. I am especially appreciative of the pastors who served there when I was in my teens. The Rev. Herb Zebarth was the pastor who first suggested that I consider entering the ordained ministry. Although it was some years later before I made that decision, he started me thinking seriously about the ministry.

The laity of that congregation also should be thanked for surrounding me with Christian love and concern. After the death of my father when I was only twelve years old, the church truly became my extended family. My Sunday school teacher and my scoutmaster really became surrogate fathers for me. One reason I became a minister was because the church, as represented by this congregation, was such a positive influence in my life.

Teachers in college and seminary helped shape my thinking and broadened my knowledge. In seminary I was forced to examine what I believed, resulting in a more enlightened and mature faith. The fact that my seminary experience was so meaningful to me made it less difficult for me to leave the parish ministry in order to enter the ministry of teaching in a theological seminary.

Parishioners in the churches I have served, colleagues in parish ministry, and seminary colleagues, along with a countless number of students, have enriched my life and stimulated my thinking. I have been privileged to be a learner even as I have endeavored to be a good teacher. I have received ministry *from* others as I have ministered *to* others, and for this I give thanks.

In regard to this book, some specific words of appreciation must be expressed. My wife, Mary Lou, and our two sons, Kirk and Paul, have taught me much about ministry and have encouraged me to persevere in this writing project. I am grateful to the Iliff School of Theology, and especially to President Donald E. Messer and Academic Dean Jane I. Smith, for granting me the sabbatical leave that enabled me to write this book. Approval for the leave was also voted by the Faculty Personnel Committee and the Iliff Board of Trustees. The Penrose Library of the University of Denver graciously allowed me the use of a faculty study room for ten months, giving me a place where I could work undisturbed.

The willingness of David Jaeger to serve as interim director of the Office of Ministerial Studies during my leave enabled me to focus my time on research and writing. The competent way in which he carried out his duties made it much easier for me to return as director upon the conclusion of my leave. My secretary Lucile Schweppe, deserves enormous thanks for taking my handwritten material and typing the first-draft manuscript. Gene Crytzer, of the Iliff secretarial staff, also did some typing of the manuscript. Finally, I am very grateful for the assistance of Tim Staveteig, and of Cynthia Thompson of Fortress Press. Their words of encouragement and advice were extremely important in the development and completion of this project.

1

The Minister as a Caring Person

"P eople don't care how much you know until they know how much you care." Those words on a small sign above a secretary's desk caught my eye as I walked through the office area of a mountain resort. The author of the words was not identified on the sign. However, the meaning was obvious and the truth profound. Surely, I thought to myself, these words are as important for a pastor and teacher as they are for a secretary. In fact, anyone whose work involves dealing with people, and that includes most of us, should heed these words. People want to know that they matter, that who they are as persons is important.

Love and Caring

If ever a word has been twisted and tortured and misused, it must be the word *love*. The word is used so casually and superficially that the profound meaning of the word can be forgotten. Someone remarked that sometimes when an individual says to another person, "I love you," what the first person really means is "I love me and want you." Selfishness does sometimes seem to dominate present-day relationships between persons.

For a better appreciation of the meaning of love, recall the numerous references to love in the New Testament. Jesus talked about God's love for the world, as evidenced by the giving of God's son (John 3:16). In his conversation with his disciples prior to his betrayal, Jesus said "This is my commandment, that you love one another as I have loved you" (John 15:12).

1

The Pharisees tried to test Jesus by asking him, "Teacher, what is the great commandment in the law?" Jesus responded by saying, "'You shall love the Lord your God with all your heart, and with all your soul, and with all your mind.' This is the great and first commandment. And a second is like it, 'You shall love your neighbor as yourself'" (Matthew 22:34-40). Jesus even admonished, "Love your enemies and pray for those who persecute you" (Matthew 5:44).

While the English language has the one word, *love,* the Greeks had three different words to differentiate between various love relationships. The word *eros* refers to romantic or sexual love. The word from which we get our word *filial* refers to the love between parent and child or to brotherly and sisterly love. The word *agape* describes the self-giving, even sacrificial love or caring that one person might express to another. This latter kind of love is what Jesus demonstrated so powerfully in his death on the cross.

Remember the great commandment that Jesus gave in his reply to the Pharisees—we are to love God. Then Jesus added a second commandment—to "love your neighbor as yourself." One of the ways we express our love for God is by loving our neighbor. That, we know, can be a difficult assignment. It may be much easier to love unknown people in a distant land than a next-door neighbor. That next-door neighbor may be someone who has a barking dog, a neglected yard, and a teenager who plays loud music on a stereo.

Expressing our love in words may be important, but our actions must reinforce our words. Do you remember the conversation that Jesus had with Peter on the beach as recorded in John 21? Peter is asked three times in succession by Jesus, "Do you love me?" Peter was annoyed at being asked the same question three times. Maybe Jesus was remembering that after Jesus was arrested it was Peter who three times denied being a disciple of Jesus (John 18:15-27). Be that as it may, Peter answered Jesus affirmatively each time the question was asked. Each time after Peter responded, assuring Jesus that he loved him, Jesus gave Peter a command. "Feed my lambs." "Tend my sheep." "Feed my sheep." The final words of Jesus to Peter were "Follow me" (John 21:15-19). The implications of the conversation are clear. Words are important but words alone are not enough. Love declared must also be love demonstrated. Actions and words must be consistent, must reinforce one another.

There is a difference between liking someone and expressing love and care toward someone. It may be impossible for a minister to like everyone to whom he or she must relate. Yet the minister must offer loving concern for each person, difficult as that may be.

Even parents who truly love their children sometimes have trouble liking them or at least liking their actions. However, I remember a psychologist saying, "It is at those times when your child is most disagreeable that the child needs your love the most." Perhaps that is true in the pastor-parishioner relationship as well. There are reasons people behave as they do, and if we are able to discover those reasons we may be able to relate more positively to the person. There may be something that happened to the person, totally unrelated to the church or the pastor, that negatively affects the relationship of the person to both church and pastor. There is an old French proverb that is worth remembering: "One who knows all, forgives all."

The Caring Ministry of Jesus

The ministry of Jesus was a profoundly caring ministry. If I were asked to choose one word to describe the ministry of Jesus, it would be the word "compassion." The word compassion is sometimes defined as sympathetic feeling or pity, but it literally means to bear or suffer with another person who is suffering. The compassionate person so identifies with the suffering of another person that the compassionate one also bears the suffering. The word "empathy" picks up something of this same meaning.

Over and over again in the Gospels we see Jesus responding to individual human need. In the Gospel of Luke, note how frequently Jesus stopped to help a person in need. In just three chapters we read that the healing touch of our Lord was directed to:
- the man who had an unclean spirit of an unclean demon (Luke 4:33-36)
- Simon's mother-in-law ill with a high fever (Luke 4:38-39)
- those who were sick with various diseases (Luke 4:40-41)
- a man full of leprosy (Luke 5:12-14)
- a man who was paralyzed (Luke 5:18-26)
- a tax collector named Levi (Luke 5:29-32)
- a man whose right hand was withered (Luke 6:6-11)

A very interesting series of sermons could be preached on "a congregation of one," looking at those numerous occasions when Jesus stopped to deal with the one person who seemed most in need of his loving concern and healing touch. Sometimes these individuals interrupted Jesus in his ministry of teaching and preaching. Jesus had time for persons whom the rest of society ignored or even scorned. Jesus even healed on the Sabbath, much to the indignation of the ruler of the synagogue (Luke 13:10-17) and to the dismay of the Pharisees (Luke 14:1-6).

In his teaching, as well as by his actions, Jesus emphasized the importance of the individual. Consider chapter 15 of Luke. In response to the criticism of the Pharisees and scribes, who "murmured" that Jesus "receives sinners and eats with them," Jesus told three parables. They are commonly known as the parables of the lost sheep, the lost coin, and the lost (prodigal) son. Although the shepherd has ninety-nine other sheep, the shepherd is greatly concerned when one is lost. He seeks the lost sheep until he finds it and then rejoices.

Likewise, the woman who has ten silver coins and loses one seeks diligently until she finds it. She, too, calls her friends and neighbors to rejoice with her at finding the coin. The parable we usually call the parable of the prodigal son could also be described as the parable of the loving father. When the repentant son returns after squandering his inheritance in a far country, the Scriptures tell us the father "had compassion, and ran and embraced him and kissed him" (Luke 15:20). A party celebrating the son's return soon gets underway.

In each of these parables Jesus emphasizes the importance of caring for not only the many but for the one. This is the attitude that all who profess to be followers of the Christ must strive to maintain. By his actions and his words, Jesus makes it very clear that this is our mandate, whether we be clergy or laity.

The Person of the Minister

The ministry is a profession where the personal characteristics of the minister, as well as basic skills, are extremely important. In the pastoral ministry, person and performance are inextricably linked. People are very concerned about who the minister is, as well as how capable the minister is in fulfilling responsibilities. The ability to relate positively to a variety of people has a lot to do with the personhood of the pastor.

To answer the question, What are the most significant characteristics people look for in a young minister or priest, one of the most comprehensive studies of the ministry ever conducted was undertaken in 1974 by the Association of Theological Schools and funded by the Lilly Endowment, Inc. "Service without regard for acclaim" received the highest ranking. Ranked second was "personal integrity." The third highest factor had to do with Christian example, being "a person that people in the community can respect." Not until we get to fourth place do we find mention of specific pastoral skills. This factor describes a person "who shows competence and responsibility by completing tasks, by being able to handle differences of opinions and who senses the need to continue to grow in pastoral skills."[1]

The word *minister* is both a noun and a verb. When it is used as a verb, it means "to serve," which implies that all Christians could be called ministers because they are all called to serve. In fact, some ordained leaders of congregations will speak of themselves as pastors and all the members of the congregation as ministers. However, in this book the words *minister* and *pastor* will be used interchangeably and will refer to the clergy who serve as the designated leaders of a congregation.

The first section of this book looks at the personal characteristics and skills needed for effective ministry. The pastor needs to be a caring person who knows how to lead, to plan and organize, to communicate, to teach, and to celebrate.

The second section of the book then looks at the practice of ministry as these necessary skills are applied to the program responsibilities of the pastor. The activities of the church, such as worship, preaching, pastoral care, administration, evangelism, and education, are discussed.

The final section of the book discusses the resources available to assist the minister in the practice of ministry. The maintenance of the minister's own physical, intellectual, and spiritual well-being is discussed in this section.

The Minister as Caregiver

In one of the classic pioneer books in the area of pastoral care, *Psychology of Pastoral Care*, Paul E. Johnson points out that a newly appointed pastor on the day of arrival has to decide where to start his or her ministry. One option is to decide that there are numerous problems to be solved, such as financial and budgetary needs or an inadequate church building needing repairs and furnishings. The pastor can be extremely busy working at these problems, but the danger of a problem-centered approach to ministry is that the real needs of the people may be neglected.

Johnson recommends a person-centered approach to pastoral work because "personal growth is more important than any problem. . . . To begin with the person is to focus on (this person's) growth as the real aim."[2] While Johnson speaks of person-centered counseling, the principle can be applied to a pastor's total ministry.

Johnson emphasizes the caregiving aspect of ministry. "A pastor is a religious leader who understands and individually cares for his (or her) people to whom they return for the health of their souls." Although the pastor is not the only caregiver in the congregation, Johnson is saying that as an individual, the pastor must accept the obligation of caring for the people of the congregation. The pastor cannot delegate this responsibility to others and thus be absolved of personal responsibility. As Johnson puts it, "The care of souls is the vocation of the Christian pastor. Every person, whatever (that person's) condition, is a claim upon (the pastor) for compassion and aid, spiritual and physical."[3]

Those who respond to God's call to be a minister must recognize that they are being called to a ministry of caring. In fact, the reason some people enter the professional ministry is because they do care. They see and feel the injustice, the evil, the pain and suffering in our world so strongly that they feel compelled to enter a profession that enables them to express their concern and bring some measure of healing and aid.

Surely the ministry offers the opportunity to care. At times it may seem that everything the minister does is expressing care, whether it be in evangelism, or preaching, or Christian education, or administration, or (more obviously, perhaps) counseling.

Many people in our world today are hurting. That has always been the case, but the media, especially television, have made us much more aware of what terrible things can happen to people. The list of problems seems endless: unemployment, substance abuse, famine, poverty, homelessness, illness, and crimes of violence. Natural disasters, such as earthquakes, hurricanes, and floods bring misery and even death. In addition to these dramatic problems, there is the stress of everyday living. A problem becoming more prevalent is loneliness. As people live longer, they often find themselves living alone, sometimes far from their extended family. Many elderly people are in nursing homes, unable to care for themselves.

Because there is so much need in the world and we are constantly told about it, there is a danger that we will become so overwhelmed that we try to put all needs out of our minds. We simply cannot respond to all the needs of people and to all the appeals made to us. Thus, what we have to do is be selective and choose a few needs or causes to which we can respond. The minister has the difficult task of maintaining the attitude of caring, while accepting the fact that all needs cannot be met. Surely the needs within the congregation the minister serves must have priority.

The pastor not only needs to be a caring person but must also motivate others to care. Some people seem just naturally to care for others, but others in the congregation need to be encouraged and trained to be care givers. One function of the ordained clergy is to equip and support the lay people in their ministry, maybe to help the "saints" really become saints. For example, lay people can be enlisted to take the tape recording of the Sunday service to shut-ins unable to attend worship. Through this ministry, people who are confined to their home or perhaps to their room can still feel a sense of belonging to a group of people who remember them and care about them.

The minister should not overlook the care giving resources available in the community. Referrals can be made and cooperative planning and programming can take place. The minister needs to be aware of these agencies, institutions, and groups beyond the church, making it a point to get acquainted with their leadership and programs.

Caring and Intimacy

While the role of the pastor as a counselor and caregiver is vital, there is a danger that the relationship between the caregiver and the person receiving care may become too intimate. This possibility must be guarded against from the very beginning of any relationship. It is clear that the responsibility for keeping the relationship from becoming too intimate rests upon the pastor.

All of us have heard or read of incidents in which persons in positions of trust have betrayed that trust by entering into relationships that went far beyond the professional relationship. Teachers, counselors, attorneys, physicians, and other professionals have been guilty of such misconduct, and unfortunately clergy have been as well. Sometimes the professional will try to defend such conduct by saying that this was a relationship between two consenting adults or that the other person was the seducer. However, the person in authority will usually be judged to be the guilty one.

The pastor is called to be a "professional" caregiver in that he or she must adhere to high standards of practice. The pastor must be sincere in expressions of caring by words and actions but at the same time must guard against overstepping boundaries.

PART 1
Personal Skills

2

Communicating

Communication is taking place all the time. It is so much a part of living that we take it for granted. The electronic media have enormously increased the amount of communication that we receive. We may wake up to the sounds of a clock radio at our bedside and listen to the news on the radio or watch it on TV as we eat breakfast. Perhaps we are also glancing at the morning newspaper at the same time. Communication has become for us a multimedia event. Throughout the day there are telephone calls, personal conversations, and meetings, with perhaps some time reserved for reading, reflection, and prayer. After an evening meeting our day may end as it began, as we catch the late news or a late night talk show on TV.

It is little wonder that phrases like "communication explosion" or "input overload" have been used to describe what is happening to us today. Television now has fifteen-second commercials, so four commercial messages can be placed before our eyes in only one minute. Cable television allows us to choose from a myriad of channels, day or night. Some TV sets even offer a split image so you can preview what is on another channel or watch two channels simultaneously. Computers can be programmed to communicate with one another.

In a world in which we are saturated with information and bombarded by more messages than we can reasonably be expected to comprehend, the church must still be about its task of communicating the gospel. If the pastor is the designated leader of the local church, then the pastor has to be an effective communicator. Competence in communication has been rated as one of the top needs of pastors by the Academy of Parish Clergy.[1] Ideas will not get translated into programs and programs will not happen unless real communication takes place.

While some persons seem more gifted than others in public speaking or writing, communication skills can be learned and enhanced. One of the joys in teaching courses in preaching and worship is to see the remarkable improvement that some students make. Often the students surprise themselves with their growth in self-confidence and speaking ability.

The Communication Process

In order for us to improve our communication skills, it is helpful to understand the communication process. While communication theory can be simplified to some extent in various diagrams, it is really a highly complex event. The influences upon each person's life, whether those influences be cultural, economic, financial, educational, or familial, affect how we communicate and how we receive communication. What we say is not always what people hear. And what we say or what people believe we said may not be what we intended to say.

One of the simplest diagrams of the communications process, one that has been around for some time, is the Shannon-Weaver model. The model was developed by Claude Shannon and Warren Weaver in research they conducted at Bell Telephone Laboratories. Although designed to study what goes on in technological communication, it is useful as a basis for understanding the elements of human interaction in any communication event.[2]

Shannon-Weaver Model

Let us assume the source is a person, and the destination is the person or persons for whom the communication is intended. The source, the sender of the message, needs to encode the message in some way, so it will be understood by the receiver. The encoding might involve words, actions, or objects. The signal is the directed energy that carries the message. This could be electrical—such as the telephone, radio, or television—or mechanical, as in the case of the human voice or a written communication. The receiver of the signal must be able to decode it to understand what the sender or source is attempting to say. Thus, it is important that the source frame the message in such a way that it can be decoded as easily as possible. To take an extreme example, if the speaker to a group speaks only English and the group only understands Spanish, there is a serious communication problem. Someone who knows both languages is needed to be the translator who decodes the message.

The destination of the communication is the intended audience or receiver of the message. This could be the person sitting next to you at lunch, a salesperson trying to sell you something, members of a club to which you belong, the congregation at worship, or any of an unlimited number of possibilities.

Knowledge and awareness of the destination by the source and, likewise, of the source by the destination are important to effective communication. If the speaker and audience know something about each other, the message is more likely to be heard and received. It is obvious, but nonetheless important, that the speaker must keep the audience in mind when preparing and delivering the message. Equally important are the destination's expectations. Have you had the experience of feeling rather apathetic while waiting for a lecture or sermon to begin? The person who is to speak is a stranger to you and you are not sure that what this person will say will really interest you. But when the speaker is introduced, suddenly you find yourself very interested, even excited about what you are about to hear. Some things are said about the speaker that intrigue you. Maybe there is something in your past that you have in common with the speaker. In any event, you now know something about the speaker and this person no longer seems a total stranger to you. Some bonding has taken place. Whether that bonding is strengthened or weakened will depend to a large extent upon the content and delivery of the message.

Another model that helps us understand the dynamic nature of the communication process was devised by David K. Berlo. Berlo may have been influenced by the Shannon-Weaver model because Berlo also uses the word "source" rather than sender. Berlo elaborates upon each component of his model in a way that suggests the complexity of the communication process.[3]

The source is the person or persons sending the message. That person's communication skills, as well as attitudes and knowledge, will all shape the message. The social system, group, or church to which the source or sender is related and the status of the person in the system

Berlo's SMCR Model

Source	Message	Channel	Receiver
Communication Skills	Elements	Seeing	Communication Skills
Attitudes	Structure	Hearing	Attitudes
Knowledge	Content	Touching	Knowledge
Social System	Treatment	Smelling	Social System
Culture	Code	Tasting	Culture

affect the communication that takes place. If the source is the minister, there may be more authority attached to the message. However, if the minister is perceived negatively by the receiver of the message, that also affects the reception of and reaction to the message.

Not only does the source relate to a particular social system, but also the sender is part of a larger culture and must communicate according to standards set by the culture. For example, radio and television stations are expected to consider cultural standards in regard to the language used and pictures shown. (Critics say the standards are being lowered.) Likewise a preacher must think about cultural standards in the use of words and examples in the sermon and in other communication.

A message is what is transmitted between source and receiver, and it is made up of various elements, such as words, ideas, pictures, music, or an object or objects of some kind. Flowers along with some words on a greeting card might form the structure of the message. The precise content of the message needs to be determined, and then the sender must choose the form or forms the message should have in order to best communicate.

When communicating we need to consider what channel or channels should be used. As indicated in the Berlo model, messages are received through all five senses, namely seeing, hearing, smelling, touching, tasting. More than one channel can be used, as in the case of the sacraments of Baptism and the Eucharist, where all the senses are involved. Such variables as our relationship to the other person, as well as time, distance, cost, and urgency will help determine the appropriate channel or channels. Sometimes a telephone call may be better than a face-to-face contact or vice versa. Sometimes the message may be best delivered alone, whereas in a different situation, having another person accompany you may bring a positive response.

It is a mistake to depend exclusively on one means of communication. Suppose the minister and the board of trustees agree that there should be a spring cleanup day at the church. A date is decided upon and the trustee meeting is adjourned. However, nothing is said about how the event will be publicized and who will be responsible for publicity. The minister assumes the chairperson of the trustees will handle this, but the chairperson assumes that since the minister was at the meeting and knows about it, the minister will announce it. A week before the scheduled cleanup day, the minister realizes no announcement has been made and puts a notice in the bulletin. Only a few people show up for the cleanup day, and the minister and the trustee chairperson are frustrated and annoyed with one another.

Had good planning and communication taken place, the event could have been a great success. Instead of relying on one printed announcement in the bulletin, a brief article could have appeared in the church newsletter, postcards could have been sent, telephone calls made, several posters could have been prepared, and perhaps the trustee chairperson could have made a personal appeal during the announcement time on Sunday morning. Using multiple channels of communication is likely to be more effective than using only one channel. Remember that the message will be heard and remembered by more people if it is presented in more than one way and more than one time.

What has been said about the source can also be applied to the receiver. The communication skills of the receiver both in listening and in sending messages will strongly affect the communication process. The other aspects listed, such as attitudes, knowledge, social system, and culture may also be influential in determining the outcome of the communication taking place.

We as human beings communicate with one another in at least three ways—speech, writing, and actions. "Actions" generally refers to non-verbal or even visual communication. Keeping in mind the role of the minister, let us briefly consider these three basic ways human beings communicate.

Speaking

When a baby begins to make sounds that seem to approximate words, how excited the parents become. To hear "mama" or "dada" from one's own little child is indeed thrilling. Then as the child begins to use other words and even form short sentences, the parents are even more delighted.

We may sometimes forget what a tremendous gift we have in this ability to form words and communicate with one another. It is again something we take for granted. However, if you have ever lost the use of your voice for a short time, you are well aware of the limitations placed upon you. Being in a foreign country and not able to speak the language of that country can bring about similar feelings.

In recent years it has been determined through careful research that each human voice is unique. No other person has a voice completely identical to your own; similar, perhaps, but not identical. Through electronic means, it is possible to make a voiceprint of an individual. Just as your fingerprint is unique, so is your voiceprint. In fact, in 1966 in New York State a voiceprint was admitted as evidence in a court of law.[4]

Even though using our voices seems to come to us naturally, being called upon to speak to a group can cause great anxiety. Often people say that their greatest fear is having to speak in public. The phrase that is sometimes used to describe what happens to these people is that they become "tongue tied." The words will not come out of their mouths, or if some words do come out, they are not well spoken. Another phrase sometimes used by actors and musicians is "performance anxiety."

Why is public speaking such an intimidating, threatening, fear-inspiring experience? Here are some possible reasons:

People who rarely do any public speaking are more likely to be fearful and nervous. While the nervousness may never totally go away for anyone, familiarity with the task does make one more comfortable with it. In fact, a certain amount of tension may be necessary to give one the energy to speak with emotion and enthusiasm. Think of holding a piece of paper between the thumb and the forefinger. You can squeeze the paper so tightly that your hand quivers and the paper shakes. Or you can relax the thumb and forefinger so much that the piece of paper falls to the floor. However, if you pick up the paper and hold it with just enough pressure, you will keep it in place. While this analogy is not perfect, it does suggest there is a middle position somewhere between being totally uptight and totally relaxed (to the point of complacency or indifference). It is this middle position that we must seek to attain in public speaking.

You must accept yourself before you can give yourself away. In preaching or any public speaking, you become the object of public scrutiny.

People look at you. Remember Jesus going to the synagogue in Nazareth, reading from the book of the prophet Isaiah, and then speaking to the people. Luke's Gospel says that "the eyes of all in the synagogue were fixed on him" (Luke 4:20). That's the feeling you get when you get up to speak. All eyes are fixed on you. It's up to you to take control of the situation, to say what you want to say or what needs to be said (they may not be the same).

A lot of self-disclosure takes place in public speaking. The words you say and the way you say them reveal something about you. If you know that what you are saying will not please some of the people, the task becomes doubly difficult. The clothes you are wearing, the gestures you use, your facial expressions, your posture all communicate something to the audience or congregation. Can you accept the fact that this communication is taking place, in ways you intended or did not intend it should take place?

Jesus said we are to love God and then love our neighbor as ourself. That statement implies that we are to love ourselves as well as God and neighbor. Sometimes we have trouble loving ourselves. We know only too well our sins and shortcomings, our physical imperfections. We have trouble accepting ourselves, to say nothing about loving ourselves. We have difficulty seeing ourselves as worthy of God's love and even more difficulty becoming channels of God's love. We think, "Who am I to stand up in front of these people and tell them what to believe and how to live? What are they thinking about me? Will they reject me? Will they be angry at what I say? Do I have anything to say worthy of their time and attention?"

These are some of the questions that may go through the mind of the minister when called upon to speak. The minister must come to terms with such questions and self-doubts and trust God's grace and love. The minister must feel accepted by God and then have sufficient self-acceptance and self-esteem to accept the role and the task of proclaiming God's word.

Focusing on the message instead of yourself as the messenger can reduce anxiety. If you have observed something or heard something of tremendous importance, you are anxious to share that news. There is an urgency that compels you to speak. The words tumble out without hesitation or nervousness. You know how important your message is, and you forget about yourself and how you look. You simply want to deliver the message. Something like that needs to happen to the minister or to anyone engaged in public speaking. The person speaking needs to be convinced of the importance of the message. Instead of being self-conscious and nervous, concentrate on the message.

Public speaking skills can be improved. Someone once remarked that the largest room in the world is the room for improvement. We all live in that room. Public-speaking skills can be improved if one is willing to acknowledge the need for improvement and work hard to make that improvement.

How can you tell if there is a problem with your public speaking? Sometimes people will tell you, especially if you arrange opportunities for them to give you feedback and evaluation. Even if people do not give you negative feedback, there are at least three aspects of public speaking that indicate a problem.

1. The manner of speaking might call attention to itself. When the listeners begin thinking about the way the speaker is speaking rather than listening to the speech, there is a problem. Sometimes this happens when the speaker has an unusual accent, such as someone with a different native language. Even the same language is spoken differently in different places. When I served as an interim pastor for about six months in England, initially the people kept mentioning my American accent. People from the northern or western United States who visit or move to the south are introduced to a southern drawl. Regional and national differences may pose problems, but mannerisms in speech or gestures can also direct the attention of the listener away from the content of the message.

2. The manner of speaking might interfere with good communication. Some of the common faults of speech may be the result of ignorance, indifference, or laziness in speaking. Some people fail to pronounce words correctly and thus are misunderstood. Once I heard a radio announcer talk about the season of "eppa fanny." I finally figured out that he was referring to that season in the Christian year called Epiphany. Keep a dictionary handy and make sure you know the correct pronunciation of a word.

Articulation of each syllable is extremely important. In casual conversation people often tend to drop word endings, saying "goin" or "gonna" instead of "going." The "th" sound becomes "ta" or "da," and the "er" sound becomes "uh" or "ah." For example, someone might say "Dat's da [that's the] time we have dinnah [dinner]. While articulation may not be much of a problem in one-on-one conversation, it becomes acutely important in a group setting. Volume alone does not help much if words are not clearly articulated.

3. The speaker may be unduly nervous. This may lead to a problem somewhat related to the problem of sloppy articulation—the habit of telescoping words. The speaker speaks too rapidly and runs the words together in a sentence without any pause between words. So "I'm going to take a walk" becomes "I'mgonnatakeawalk."

Other problems in public speaking include a lack of variety in pitch and inflection, resulting in a monotonous pattern of speaking. Some people, especially those reading from a manuscript, fade in volume toward the end of each sentence. Listeners who have some hearing loss find this particularly annoying. What apparently happens is that before finishing the sentence, the speaker looks down to anticipate the next sentence. The speaker then is psychologically disengaging from the first sentence, and this is reflected in voice and volume. If the speaker maintains eye contact to the end of the sentence, that will help sustain volume as well.

Writing

Words are one of the ways we communicate, whether the words are spoken or written. Words are one of the minister's most important tools and the competent minister must learn to use them well.

The minister is often involved in communication through writing. There are letters to write to parishioners, prospective members, colleagues, and friends. If the church publishes a newsletter, the minister in a small church may need to do most of the writing for it, while in a larger church the minister will at least write a column and perhaps one or two articles. Some ministers write a column for the local newspaper. The minister may write articles or even books for publication.

The preparation of the worship service involves writing. Even if the minister does not read the sermon from a manuscript, the minister may write it out in full in order to organize material and be better prepared. Other parts of the worship service may require original writing, such as the call to worship, prayers, or announcements. Other public speaking occasions will require writing in anticipation of what one will say. Writing up notes of pastoral care or counseling sessions can be helpful, especially if the sessions are ongoing. Denominational and local church reports will be required. Keeping a personal journal can be a helpful support for one's spiritual life.

Computers and word processors have made the writing task of the minister easier and perhaps even more enjoyable. Judging by the high number of seminary students who are computer literate and even own their own computers, it appears most of the ministers of the future will own and use a computer. If you have not yet made friends with a computer, you should consider doing so.

In addition to learning to use a computer, there are three other steps you can take to improve your writing:

Make writing a part of your preparation for speaking. Writing takes time, and time is a precious commodity for ministers as well as other people. Because many ministers are quite verbal, and talk comes easy for them, they are tempted to avoid using writing as a means of preparation. The minister, pressed for time or wanting to give something else a higher priority, decides to wing it. While one may get by with this on some occasions, it is a dangerous practice. Eventually it could cause some serious problems. Do not shortchange writing as a part of your preparation for public speaking, preaching, and other leadership roles.

Make sure your writing makes a favorable first impression. Your writing communicates something about you, the writer, as well as about the content of the writing. The format in which your writing is presented, as well as the words you choose and the thoughts you share, are significant in forming an overall impression.

A retired minister once told me that during most of his ministry he had personally typed the bulletins for the worship services he conducted. "Didn't you have a secretary or someone in the congregation who could do that for you?" I asked.

"Oh yes, I did, but since the bulletin gives people their first impression of the worship experience, I wanted that bulletin to be as close to perfect as it could be. If there were any mistakes in it, they were mine and I couldn't blame anyone else."

I do not commend this minister for doing all the work on the bulletin himself, but I do admire his concern to have the worship bulletin create the most favorable impression possible.

Make good writing a priority in your ministry. If you already have good writing skills, be thankful and make good use of those skills. If there are some weaknesses in your writing skills, determine what they are and try to correct them. Perhaps you can enroll in a writing workshop or course. Perhaps you can arrange for some private instruction and tutoring if that will help you. Sometimes just reviewing the basic rules of grammar can be helpful. If you are not using a computer with spell-check capabilities and spelling is a problem for you, have someone else proofread any written communication that goes to the public. Keep a dictionary and a thesaurus handy so you use words correctly both in writing and speaking.

Just as in public speaking, consider your audience when you write. Use words, images and examples that will be meaningful to those receiving your written communication. If you are preparing something to be delivered orally, such as a lecture, speech, or sermon, remember to use language suitable for oral delivery. That may mean using shorter sentences and even shorter words.

Do not overlook the value of sending brief thank-you notes to people who have made some special contribution of time, talent, or possession to the church. Think how meaningful it would be to someone to receive a short, handwritten note from their pastor. Most of us do not say "thank you" often enough. Of course, you can also say thank you or offer congratulations by using the telephone. This method may be quicker unless you get into an extended conversation, and it is personal. However, sometimes the person you are calling is not there and you talk to an answering machine. Or maybe you just do not try phoning again and the message never gets delivered. At least the written note is likely to be received, and some people may want to keep it and look at it again rather than throw it away.

Nonverbal Communication

Reuel Howe, in a newsletter of the Institute of Pastoral Studies, tells of visiting a friend in Brazil. While walking through the city together, they came upon a small crowd of people listening to a street corner preacher. The preacher was speaking in Portuguese, a language Dr. Howe did not understand. After listening to the preacher for a while, Dr. Howe turned to his friend and asked, "What is he saying?"

"He's preaching about the love of God," was the reply.

"I never would have guessed that," said Reuel Howe.[5]

Why did Dr. Howe respond as he did? The facial expression, manner of speaking, gestures, and body posture of the speaker did not convey any sense of love. Instead, the speaker seemed to be expressing anger, judgment, and condemnation. The nonverbal communication contradicted the verbal communication.

When there is a contradiction between the verbal and nonverbal communication, the nonverbal is perceived to be true. If I raise my arm and shake my clenched fist at you while at the same time saying "I love you," you will not believe that my words are expressing my true feelings.

If gestures or actions are contrived rather than natural, they can become a barrier to communication. Gestures can call attention to the gestures themselves rather than to the message. Nonverbal and verbal communication need to be congruent with one another.

The minister needs to develop the ability to see the nonverbal communication expressed by the audience or person to whom the minister is speaking. If on a Sunday morning the service has been unusually long and the minister is still preaching when people normally are on their way home, there may be restless shifting of position, people glancing at their watches, and even some people leaving. The nonverbal communication is telling the minister it is time to quit.

Like it or not, the clothes the minister wears, the kind of car the minister drives, and the way the minister drives the car are all forms of nonverbal communication. A man visited a friend in a distant city and rode in the friend's car. However, the man was appalled at the friend's driving habits: the driver did not wait for pedestrians in the crosswalk; he tailgated; he cut suddenly in front of another car; he honked his horn more than seemed necessary. Not wanting to offend his host, the visitor said nothing.

About a year later the man returned and was met at the airport by his friend who was still driving the same car. Somewhat apprehensive, the man entered the car and braced himself for what he thought would be an unpleasant experience. To his surprise the driver was the best possible example of a courteous, considerate driver. He stopped to let pedestrians cross the street. At a four-way stop sign, he waved to another driver to cross ahead of him. There was no horn honking, just friendly smiles and much patience.

Amazed, the visitor said, "You know when I visited you last year I was really embarrassed by the way you drove. You didn't seem to look out for anybody but yourself. Now you are the very soul of courtesy. What has happened to you?"

"Oh," said the friend, "I thought you would notice. A few months ago a friend of mine in the city was running for election and I carried a big sign for him on top of my car. I decided if I wanted people to vote for this guy, I had to drive so people wouldn't get mad at me. That's what I did. And it was so much fun I decided to drive that way all the time."

This man had learned that communication is taking place all the time, whether we intend it to take place or not. Whether the communication be through speaking, writing, or nonverbal actions, the minister must seek to communicate as effectively and positively as possible. The minister is called to communicate the gospel in word and in deed. What a challenge that is, but what an exciting one as well.

3

Leading and Supervising

The pastor with whom I was speaking was serving a congregation involved in a building program. "How is the building program coming along?" I asked.

"Oh, I guess pretty well. We haven't approved any plans yet, and I'm not sure what the committee has in mind."

Surprised, I asked, "What do you mean, you don't know what the committee has in mind? Don't you meet with the committee?"

He replied, "Well, I met with them the first time they met, but I told them then that I thought they should meet without me so they wouldn't expect me to tell them what to do."

"That shocks me" I said. "I can't imagine a pastor not meeting with the committee responsible for planning a new church building. After all, you're supposed to be the leader of the congregation. You have training and knowledge that the laypeople don't have."

"Oh, I don't know anything about construction and building. And it's really not my church. It's their church. They'll still be there when I'm gone. They should decide what they want without me interfering."

This pastor was obviously proud of his ability to be uninvolved and to trust the laypeople on the committee to make the right decisions without him.

Another pastor came to a congregation that had been served for a few months by an interim pastor. The congregation had developed a program whereby four lay leaders of the congregation assisted in leading the worship service each Sunday on a rotating basis. The interim pastor had helped train them to improve their public-speaking skills and appreciated their help. The new pastor was there less than a month when he informed the four lay leaders that their assistance in worship was no longer needed. He told them that he had been trained in seminary to lead worship; it was something that he did well and enjoyed doing; it was part of his job description; and it had been his experience in his previous congregation that people in the congregation expected clergy and not lay persons to lead worship.

Next, the pastor informed the choir director that he was not pleased with the selection of anthems and special music. The pastor wanted what he described as "more serious church music," and said that in the future the choir director should submit all music selections to the minister for approval before they were sung in worship. Within two weeks the choir director resigned and the minister informed the music committee and then the congregation that since he had musical training, he would become the director of the choir.

Both of these pastors, whom we might call Pastor A and Pastor B, are real people. Pastor A told me his story, and the events that took place in regard to Pastor B were told to me by a member of the congregation. Let us reflect on these two contrasting leadership styles.

Pastor A believed the lay people of the congregation should make decisions regarding the building program of the church without his participation. His rationale for not meeting with the committee was that they might depend too heavily on him and thus he would exert undue influence on their decision. However, Pastor A's style of leadership was really an abdication of leadership. He had a seminary education and prior pastoral experience. He had studied worship and was the worship leader of the congregation. Surely he had some important knowledge to share with the committee, even though he may have lacked any understanding of construction procedures. His style of leadership can be best described as laissez-faire.

Pastor B represents the other extreme in leadership. He comes to the congregation apparently convinced that he knows more than anyone else about what should happen in the church, especially in regard to worship. Nobody is going to tell him what to do in planning and conducting worship. He sees himself as a strong leader, willing to take bold action. He apparently makes no attempt to engage in consultation before issuing arbitrary orders. He makes little or no use of any of the boards and committees of the church that exist to help make decisions. He calls himself a "take charge kind of guy" and sees that as a positive trait. Yet he tramples over the thoughts and feelings of others as though they do not exist. His style of leadership can only be called "authoritarian" in the most negative sense of the word.

The congregation served by Pastor A did build a new church building and it really wasn't a bad building. The committee got a lot of help from the architect they chose, and the chairperson of the committee consulted with the pastor even though the pastor did not attend the building committee meetings. However, shortly after the building was completed, the pastor decided to leave parish ministry, get more education, and go into a specialized ministry in a nonparish setting.

After he had been the minister for less than a year, the discontent with Pastor B was evident in decreased attendance at worship and in a lack of participation in the decision making groups of the church. He eventually moved to another parish, leaving a congregation smaller in membership then when he came. His successor had to bring some healing to a congregation in which at least some of the remaining members were angry and resentful.

A strength, if carried to an extreme, can become a weakness. One of Pastor A's strengths seems to be a willingness to delegate responsibility to others. He is humble about his own ability to contribute to the planning of a new church building. He is not interested in exerting his leadership in an authoritarian manner. However, these traits are so pronounced in Pastor A that they lead to what appears to be an avoidance of responsibility and a lack of leadership.

Pastor B, on the other hand, does not hesitate to claim the authority of his role as pastor. He is willing to make decisions that he believes are right even though they may be unpopular. If his decisions result in more work for him to do, he doesn't seem to mind. He exudes self-confidence. His strong ego is not easily bruised. Yet, the net result of his authoritarian style of leadership is angry, resentful parishioners who decide that if he is the leader, they do not want to be followers.

In these two pastors we have seen extremes of leadership ranging from passive to authoritarian. If these styles are likely to be ineffective in a congregation, then what is an effective style of leadership? A preferable way of leading lies somewhere in the middle of a continuum between laissez-faire leadership style at one end, and the authoritarian style at the other end. A diagram of this range of leadership styles would look something like the one at the top of page 27.

Laissez-faire	Participatory	Authoritarian

The laissez-faire style could be labeled *permissive. Democratic* or *shared* leadership are words that could be substituted for participatory. Sometimes the word *autocratic* is used in place of *authoritarian.*

There may be times when the organization or group is best served if the designated leader allows the group to work without a strong assertion of leadership on his or her part. On another occasion it may be necessary for the leader decisively to exercise his or her authority. However, most of the time it seems that a shared sense of leadership, a participatory style, will allow the group to more fully own the decisions that are made. This ownership of the decision making process results in a much greater likelihood of success in implementing whatever decision is made.

To argue for a participatory or democratic style of leadership and decision making is not to suggest that the pastor is not a leader. The pastor has special knowledge and training that needs to be made available to the people being served. Although the pastor is not the only leader of the congregation, the pastor must be the primary leader. Without effective pastoral leadership, the congregation is not likely to succeed in fulfilling its mission of "increasing among people the love of God and neighbor."[1]

Alan Sager asked several Lutheran bishops to nominate a total of twenty "particularly effective pastors." The list included rural, urban, and suburban ministries, two camping ministries, and one campus ministry. Dr. Sager interviewed each of these pastors. After reviewing and reflecting upon his notes from these visits, Dr. Sager listed twenty characteristics that frequently were evident in these pastors who were leading effective ministries. The very first characteristic noted by Dr. Sager referred to the leadership role of the pastor. As Dr. Sager stated it, "Effective pastors see themselves as leaders; they are willing to be upfront, strong leaders as may be necessary." Dr. Sager goes on to say that "in recent years the talented, trained, and experienced have been under pressure . . . to conceal their competence in the interest of extending democracy. We have been claimed and 'had' by the romantic notion that anybody's word is as good as anyone else's word on any subject. Excellence has been dethroned. Mediocrity is king. To change the figure, no one is at the wheel."[2]

Dr. Sager says that some of the pastors he interviewed believe that the abdication of leadership in the church is due in part to "the assumption . . . that a minister is there only to do full time what a lay person can do only part time. The difference is quantitative not qualitative, say those who deny the uniqueness of pastoral leadership. The effective pastors noted that the priesthood of all believers was never intended to un-priest the responsibly ordained."[3]

Furthermore, these pastors believe that "more churches have been hurt by pastoral default than have ever been hurt by pastoral domination." While that may be true, both pastoral default and pastoral domination are unhealthy expressions of leadership. Dr. Sager's closing comment about the importance of service as a characteristic of leadership is that these pastors see themselves as "serving by leading."[4] There is no tension for them between serving and leading. To lead is to serve.

Dr. Sager's research emphasizing the crucial importance of pastoral leadership is supported by the writings of R. Robert Cueni. In his book *The Vital Church Leader,* Dr. Cueni says flatly that "the health of the congregation rises or falls based on the levels of commitment and competence of its minister; and on the quality of the relationship established between that person and the members of the church."[5]

One could argue that factors other than pastoral leadership can influence the health of a congregation. Major demographic changes, such as population shifts, can affect the membership trends. For example, a congregation located in a rapidly growing suburb is in an entirely different situation than a small rural church in a county where the population is declining. However, the essential truth of Cueni's statement remains. "Study the fifty-year history of any congregation," he says. "When plotting numerical, financial, outreaching, and programmatic 'highs,' almost without exception, one discovers that these times came when the church was served by its most effective ministers. And leadership skills made those ministers effective."[6]

Perhaps Cueni's most convincing argument is that if one studies the ministries of these same pastors in other settings, "one discovers that ministers who are effective in one congregation are effective in others."[7] The question we must address is, What qualities, characteristics, or skills are necessary for a minister to be an effective leader? While many characteristics and skills could be noted, I want to highlight just three at this point. The effective pastoral leader must accept the responsibilities of being a role model, a visionary, and a spiritual leader.

Role Model

Like it or not, the pastor of a congregation is often looked upon as a *role model* for other persons. Oftentimes, if the pastor is married and has a family, the spouse and the children are expected to be role models as well. This may seem unfair to the family, but it does happen. Ask almost any PK (preacher's kid) what that feels like and you are likely to get a negative response.

The pastor needs to do some interpretation for the congregation regarding the role expectations being placed upon the pastor and family. The pastor-parish relations committee, or some similar group in a local church, can help a great deal by being a communicator and mediator between pastor and congregation. The pastor should be able to use such a committee for guidance in these matters.

Even though congregations seem to be giving more freedom to ministers and their families to live their own lives, the pastor is a public figure, much like a person holding public office. If a minister gets into difficulty with the law, the news of that is much more likely to appear in the local newspaper than if a less well-known person is involved. The pastor is considered to be one of the leaders of a community and therefore subject to public scrutiny. Privileges are often extended to the clergy by congregation and community, but those privileges also bring responsibilities.

Since this role model expectation is placed upon the minister, why not accept it as graciously as possible and seek to be a positive example? To do so is not easy because it means avoiding even the appearance of wrongdoing, as well as wrongdoing itself. People often tend to expect a higher standard of conduct of the minister than they do of themselves or even of other public figures. The minister is expected to be a moral leader as well as a role model.

The concept of the pastor as moral leader is developed in an interesting way by Richard Bondi who suggests that the minister should embody the skill of story telling. Says Bondi, "Leaders hear powerful stories and tell them to those they would lead."[8] The minister tells the story from within the community but is also challenged to tell the story from the edge of the community. The pastor knows the congregation (or community) as a person within it and yet can bring an outside perspective to the congregation. If the minister's message is to be heard and accepted, the minister must be seen as an authentic person, endeavoring to live as he or she invites others to live.

While the minister may not regard a particular activity as wrong or sinful, the minister needs to consider whether other persons will be misled by observing the minister. The writer of 1 Timothy says to this young Christian, "Let no one despise your youth, but set the believers an example in speech and conduct, in love, in faith, in purity" (1 Timothy 4:12). In the second letter to Timothy the writer says that "God did not give us a spirit of cowardice, but rather a spirit of power and of love and of self-discipline" (2 Timothy 1:7).

Clergy must exercise self-discipline, living our lives as nearly as we can in the way that Christ would have us live. After all, we regard Christ as our role model, do we not? We know that we will fail at times, make mistakes, and perhaps not be the role model that the minister is expected to be. At such times we need to be honest with ourselves and others, repent and ask forgiveness, and then seek to do our best to be faithful to the high calling to which we have been called.

Visionary Leader

An ancient story tells of a king who was concerned about one of the villages in his kingdom. The homes in the village were not kept in good repair. The streets were in bad condition. Trash was thrown anywhere and everywhere. The people of the village apparently had no pride in the appearance of their village. After conferring with his advisors, the king ordered a model of the village to be made. The layout of the village was the same as the existing village but it showed the village as it could be, with attractive homes, shrubs and flowers, clean streets, and all trash removed.

The model was put in the center of the village, and the people of the village were told that the king wanted them to study it to see how their village could be improved. Some months later the king sent an ambassador to inspect the village. The ambassador came back with a glowing report. The village had changed dramatically for the good. People had seen the model and realized that their village could be different. The model that the king provided them had given them a vision of what could be and they had responded to that vision.

Just as the king provided the people of the village with a vision, so must the minister provide the congregation with a vision of what can be. The minister must be the *visionary* who looks to the future and helps the people dream dreams. Leading includes visioning.

Robert Cueni says "By offering vision, leaders shape the thinking and consequently, the doing of the congregation. The vision, therefore, not only describes the present but also points to the desired destination. By becoming the congregation's road map, the vision helps determine destiny as well as describe present reality."[9]

Unfortunately, ministers sometimes have great visions but little patience. They want too much to happen too fast. This is probably more likely to be true of beginning ministers who wonder why the congregation does not immediately accept the minister's great new idea. Pastors must realize that there will often be resistance to a vision that involves change. Visions need to be carefully presented and patiently nurtured. The vision must become a shared vision if the vision is to become a reality.

Martin Luther King Jr. was a courageous, visionary leader in the civil rights movement. He lifted up to people the possibility that their rights could be achieved through nonviolence. He gave them a sense of hope when the situation seemed to call for despair. His great "I have a dream" speech painted an eloquent vision of what could someday be reality. As people linked arms and sang "We shall overcome," their spirits were lifted and their faith was restored. They truly believed in their hearts that someday they (and the cause of justice) would overcome the evil of racism. The dream has not been fully realized but much progress has been made.

Few ministers will be involved in leading a national cause in the prominent way that Martin Luther King Jr. was. Yet the need for visioning is present in every local church and every community. The minister, because of education, prior experience, contacts with other clergy, access to community leaders, available information, outside resources, and status within the congregation and community, is well equipped to be the one who offers the vision.

This is not to say that being a visionary is exclusively reserved for clergy. The minister is not the only leader in the congregation or community. But being the pastoral leader of a congregation means envisioning the potential for positive change. The pastor needs to encourage others to share their visions, as well as to present her or his vision in such a way that it becomes a shared vision. Likewise, the pastor must test the validity of any vision, modify it as seems necessary, and develop a strategy to implement it. This happens best when the minister uses a participatory or democratic style of leadership.

Spiritual Leader

Paul Wilkes describes what he terms "the changing and often deeply troubled world of America's Protestant, Catholic, and Jewish seminaries." He notes the problems facing these major religious bodies. He asserts that a growing number of members of the Roman Catholic Church, the largest American church, "consider the church peripheral to their lives. They no longer look upon their priest, if indeed the current shortage allows them one, as a role model and spiritual leader."[10] What Wilkes says about the Catholic priests may also be true of Protestant clergy as well. If indeed a substantial number of ministers and priests are no longer seen as role models and spiritual leaders, then we do have a serious problem.

Spiritual leadership is the calling to which pastors and priests have given themselves. It is the primary reason for the existence of ordained, professional clergy. While leadership is essential in all aspects of the life of a congregation, leadership in the spiritual realm surely must rank as a top priority. Wilkes asks about the seminary students of today, "Will they become the religious leaders to whom a skeptical but—as often poll after poll confirms—spiritually hungry populace is willing to listen?"[11] The clergy of today and tomorrow must be the spiritual leaders for our society because there really are no other persons equipped to take their place.

While this issue of spiritual leadership will be addressed more adequately in chapter 14, I want to comment on it briefly here. The pastor must maintain her or his personal spirituality through quiet times of reading, meditating, and praying. Group experiences as well as renewal retreats are helpful ways to strengthen the spiritual life.

In the various leadership roles that the pastor assumes, the sense of being a spiritual leader of the congregation should be kept in mind. As the pastor leads others in worship, the pastor should also seek to worship. In teaching, organizing, or counseling, the pastor is God's person, God's representative.

Wilkes mentions that the religious leader is expected to be a role model. Persons involved in ministry are often the ones most aware of their limitations and shortcomings. As the apostle Paul stated so well, we indeed have "heavenly treasure in earthen vessels." Or, as the New Revised Standard version puts it, "We have this treasure in clay pots" (2 Corinthians 4:7). A member of a congregation is said to have remarked to the pastor, "Sir, your words terrify me, but your life reassures me." Spiritual counsel is more easily given than practiced. Yet we are called to follow the example of Christ, difficult as that may be.

Wilkes also talks about the expectations people have for this generation of seminarians:

> We want them to be people who in some tiny way reflect mercy and goodness of the God we want to know, not only his judgment. We want them to be people who see the goodness in us that we have yet to unleash, the potential within us to transcend our differences. In the end, I think, we are looking for those who will help us find that voice deep within us which is not our own, but calls us to do what is right.[12]

The Pastor as Supervisor

We have already spoken of the value of involving lay people in the caring work of ministry. Whenever a pastor does so, the pastor necessarily becomes involved in supervision. Pastors may also have the responsibility of supervising others on the church staff or interns from a theological seminary. Whatever form and level it takes, supervision can be a complex process. The word *supervision* itself comes from two words meaning "over" and "see." The supervisor is someone who oversees the activity or performance of another person or persons. The person being supervised (the supervisee) is usually accountable in some fashion to the supervisor.

Supervision may have negative connotations for some clergy because it takes time, it involves relational skills, and it requires a strong commitment on the part of the persons involved. It may require some critical or evaluative comments, perhaps in written form. It may even result in having to dismiss or remove someone from a position. No wonder some pastors prefer not to see themselves as supervisors.

However, supervision need not be seen as negative or as an obligation forced upon an unsuspecting pastor who simply wants help. We can look to the New Testament for some precedents. Did not Jesus supervise his disciples? Was not Paul a supervisor for Timothy? In Scripture the word shepherd holds some of the same meaning as the words *overseer* or *supervisor*.

Pastors need to see supervision as an integral part of their ministry. Supervision provides an opportunity to work with people in ways that can be affirming and growth producing. Supervision is a teaching process, but not in the formal sense of a classroom setting. Supervision may include aspects of pastoral care, and yet it should not be equated with extended counseling or therapy. There are elements of administration involved, but supervision is not simply assigning a task and making sure it gets done.

Perhaps a diagram will help explain what is meant by pastoral supervision.

Job Management	Pastoral Supervision	Pastoral Counseling

The emphasis of pastoral supervision is upon the performance of another person in the practice of ministry. The key words are "performance" and "person." Both words are important and must be kept in tension with one another. If performance is separated from person and overemphasized, then only job management is taking place. If person is overemphasized, then the relationship is likely to move into pastoral counseling or even therapy.

A seminary student was serving as the full-time intern pastor of a congregation whose senior pastor was noted as a counselor. When the young seminarian and his wife experienced some severe marital difficulties, without realizing what was happening, the senior pastor shifted roles. He became the marriage counselor for the intern and his wife and abandoned the supervisory role. The marriage was saved but some of the opportunity for the intern to learn about ministry was lost. Both the intern and the supervisor came to this conclusion in their final shared evaluation.

Models of Supervision

Don Beisswenger has identified seven different modes of understanding the supervisory task.[13] These included worker, instructor, apprentice, trainer, resource, consultant, and spiritual guide. The mode used in supervision may vary according to the situation, the nature of the relationship between the persons involved, and the personalities and experiences of each person. Some persons will obviously feel more comfortable with some modes of supervision than with others. In certain situations a particular mode of supervision may be more appropriate than another, and a competent supervisor will sense what that mode should be. Oftentimes a supervisor will use a composite of several modes at the same time. Any model of supervision consists of at least five dimensions:[14]

1. *Goal*—The desired outcome of the supervision. This needs to be mutually agreed upon.
2. *Task*—What must be done by supervisor and supervisee to achieve the goal.
3. *Focus of attention*—The particular activity, value, or emphasis on which attention will be concentrated.
4. *Relationship*—The primary way supervisor and supervisee will work together.
5. *Focus of control*—The person(s) in whom the decision making power resides.

Each of these aspects of supervision will vary according to the mode of supervision being used and the relationship of the persons involved.

The true test of good supervision is the relationship between supervisor and supervisee. Each person needs self-knowledge, and each one needs to know something about the other. There needs to be clarity about the relationship and the process. Only then can there be a relationship of openness and trust between them.

Supervision must be seen as an expression of ministry—the process of guiding and enabling persons to grow toward a fuller humanness, but a humanness expressed in the image of God and in a relationship of commitment to Jesus Christ as Savior. Then the purpose of supervision is to enable persons to engage in mutual ministry in such a way as to stimulate growth and develop skills.

Three vital elements in supervision are (1) the covenant or contract, (2) the supervisory conference or dialogue, and (3) the evaluation process. Let us examine how each of these might take place in a parish setting.

The Covenant or Contract

The word *covenant* reminds us of the biblical use of that word, suggesting the binding of persons in mutual trust before and with God. A contract defines precisely what the expectations and duties are for each party to the contract. Hence, both words are important.

If a student is being supervised by an experienced pastor, the term *learning covenant* is often used. The student in consultation with pastor and congregation establishes learning goals for the experience of ministry that will take place. Perhaps a better way of stating the dual nature of the student's experience is to speak of a "learning/serving" covenant or agreement. That phrase might apply to any church-related supervisory relationship because both parties are expected to learn and to serve.

As John Classen has stated, this covenant "will come about through a fair amount of energy spent with all involved in sharing hopes, reflection, dialogue and intentional setting of priorities."[15] Mutual expectations and understandings can be shared and agreed upon. Lack of clarity about these expectations, understandings, and relationships can lead to serious problems at a later time. Too often, expectations are assumed but not spelled out or clarified in a way that could prevent future misunderstanding.

For example, a church member volunteers to help put out the church newsletter. There is no mention of the length of time this volunteer may be expected to serve. Is it for three months, six months, a year or indefinitely? What if the person is a poor typist or makes numerous spelling errors? Who is responsible for supervising this person and making certain the newsletter is properly prepared and mailed? Is this person expected to recruit other volunteers and then take charge of them? What does this person expect of the pastor? What does the pastor really expect of this person?

If some of these matters are not clarified early in the process, there may indeed be trouble later. In any such relationship it is important to share mutual expectations and then arrive at some kind of contract or covenant. Perhaps the contract will be unwritten, although it might be better to have some kind of signed agreement. You may wish to call it simply a memorandum of understanding.

In larger congregations with a paid staff, job descriptions and contracts are more common, but even then there needs to be conversation about mutual expectations. For example, if the associate pastor assumes that he or she will determine how much time should be spent in the church office, and the senior pastor assumes the associate will be in the office from 8:30 A.M. to 12:00, there definitely needs to be some conversation.

The Supervisory Conference or Dialogue

In the large church where there may be two or more ordained pastors and other full-time and part-time paid staff, the weekly staff meeting is fairly common. However, the agenda of those meetings can vary greatly from church to church. Much depends on how the meetings are perceived by the senior minister, and how the senior minister sees his or her relationship to the staff. Is this a team? Is the group a "team" in word only, or is teamwork a matter of attitude and action? What is the relationship between the senior minister and the staff? How do they relate to one another? Do they talk about their relationships? Is there openness and trust? Can negative opinions be expressed and accepted?

The pastor ought also to meet regularly with staff members on an individual basis. Often people assume that because they see one another in passing or in a larger group setting there is no need for one-on-one meetings. However, some persons are reluctant to request an appointment with the supervisor unless there is a serious problem. By meeting regularly, major problems may be prevented because discussion took place early.

These supervisory conferences can be much more productive if people are prepared. There are some tools of supervision that can be utilized in the individual sessions or even in the group sessions. Some of the tools of supervision that can be used in supervisory conferences include the significant or critical incident report, the verbatim report, the case study, and the audio or video cassette. Theological reflection is another tool of supervision and will be discussed in chapter 5. A general description of each tool follows.

Significant or critical incident report. This report can be about some experience of ministry that generated strong feelings in the person writing the report. Sometimes it is helpful to recall the high point or low point of one's ministry during a period of time such as the previous week or month.

Verbatim report. This report could focus on an experience of ministry similar to one that could be written about in a significant incident report. However, the verbatim report provides all or part of a conversation or discussion that took place between one or more persons. Usually one of those persons is the one who writes the report. The writer tries to write the entire conversation word for word. If it was too lengthy, parts of it can be summarized.

Case study. This is another format that can be used to share and reflect on any kind of experience of ministry. This form allows more flexibility in the type of experience reported. There are a variety of case study outlines in use. The case study, as well as the previously mentioned report forms, allows for an exciting interchange of ideas and responses. Usually some solid inductive learning takes place as the pre-senter's act of ministry begins to be owned by the supervisor and/or other participants.

Audio or video report. An audio or video tape can be made of an event for which the person provided leadership. Such an event might be conducting worship, preaching a sermon, teaching a class, leading a meeting or even counseling a person. If a counseling session is being recorded, it should only be done with the permission of the person or persons being counseled. In fact, confidentiality needs to be considered and respected in all of these reports.

Often people are reluctant to take time to write a report to be used in a supervisory conference. "Why not just let me talk about what hap-pened?" someone may ask. Obviously, a verbal report is one way of communicating, but there is value in preparing a written report in advance of the supervisory session.

Preparation requires the person reporting to give more thought to selecting the specific experience that will be shared. When recalling the experience and writing about it, the person begins to process and evalu-ate the experience. Some good learning is already taking place. The supervisor or the person directing the session, as well as any other par-ticipants, should receive copies of the report in advance of the meeting and can then begin reflecting on the contents of the written document. Because a written report is used, the supervisory dialogue or conference becomes more focused and less time is wasted. Preparation makes the event more important and allows more learning to take place.

The Evaluation Process[16]

In recent years there has been much more emphasis placed upon the evaluation of clergy, so pastors are becoming involved in the evaluation process. However, there is often strong resistance to evaluation. We are reluctant to be evaluated or to evaluate someone else. Such reluctance is understandable, for all of us are at least somewhat aware of our imper-fections and shortcomings. We imagine the worst, and we become uneasy and defensive.

To be sure, evaluation can be negative and counterproductive, but it can also be positive and affirming. Actually, as we all know, evaluation takes place all the time, but usually it is informal and not shared with the person being evaluated.

One of the ways to remove some of the defensiveness is to ask the person being evaluated to first do some *self-evaluation*. Suppose that a colleague has asked you to evaluate a sermon he or she has preached. You could ask the preacher to provide a self-evaluation and then add your comments to that evaluation. Often individuals are more critical of themselves than others are. You, in fact, may then be able to affirm the person, as well as offer helpful suggestions for strengthening the sermon.

Another important aspect of evaluation is to enlist *the evaluation of others* who also have been somehow involved in this person's work. If you are evaluating a church school superintendent, you may ask for evaluative comments from other staff members, from the Christian Education Commission, from teachers, and pupils. Your understanding of this person's work will be informed and perhaps even corrected by what others say.

Evaluation should be *based on observable behavior*. People are much more likely to accept evaluative statements if you can point to a specific incident or example that supports your comment. Comments made without supporting evidence are not very useful and are likely to be rejected by the person to whom they are addressed.

Evaluation should be *given with the future in mind*. While we need to look at past behavior as the basis for evaluation, the primary purpose of critical evaluation is not to scold the other person but to help this person grow and improve.

Evaluation should be an *ongoing process*. If you have held regular supervisory conferences and have been open and honest with one another, you have constantly been engaged in evaluation. An overworked word, but one that has less sting to it, is *feedback*. A good supervisor tries to give helpful feedback on a regular basis and also wants to receive feedback. If you are expected to write a formal evaluation of someone you have been supervising, there really should be no surprises for the supervisee in that report.

Evaluation should *affirm the strengths* of the individual as well as point out the areas in which further growth should take place. Too often we take for granted the strengths of another person and only point to what we perceive as weaknesses. All of us need affirmation, and that needs to be verbalized to the persons we supervise.

Formal, written evaluations that may be required or at least requested often pose a problem for the person asked to prepare one. This is especially true if the supervisor believes some negative comments are necessary. If some of the suggestions made above are followed, this task becomes much less onerous. The formal evaluation should be seen as part of the learning process: in order for learning to happen the evaluation really needs to be shared with the person being evaluated. At the seminary where I teach, we ask our field supervisors to share evaluations with the student so maximum learning can take place. An alternative method, which some supervisors prefer, is to have supervisor and supervisee go through the evaluation form together, attempting to agree on what should be stated and then writing that down.

Evaluation should be a *mutual process,* a two-way street. If you supervise others and evaluate them, they should have the opportunity to give you feedback and evaluate you. In order for this to happen, you have to create a relationship of mutual trust. You need to be sure you can handle the feedback before you ask for it, and you need to provide a structure whereby the evaluation can be shared in a way that does not threaten those giving the evaluation.

Team Building

Although there is an inevitable hierarchy of leadership in local congregations, a wise pastor attempts to have the paid staff and/or key volunteers function as a team. While team building may not be directly related to supervising, it is an essential aspect of organizational development.

An effective team improves the functioning of the organization and the quality of the organization's work. Team building helps persons who work together on a task learn to work together more effectively.

The process of team building is not to be confused with group therapy or other sensitivity training. A therapy group is a training device in which personal feelings and relationships between group members are the actual agenda for the group. In team building the primary emphasis is on task accomplishment. Members' feelings and relationships will inevitably need attention but always in relation to task accomplishment. When feelings interfere with member functioning and team effectiveness, those feelings and relationships must be worked through.

As you build and work with your team, you may need to give attention to one or more of the processes listed below. This checklist of questions can be used by a team as a basis of discussion.[17] Members can be asked to check those questions they think need attention now, or will need attention soon. The results can then be shared and discussed. A follow-up discussion might suggest specific ways of making the team more effective.

1. How does this team work together? Do we tap all our members' resources? What seems to be aiding or blocking participation?

2. How well are persons listening to one another? When listening is poor, how does the group respond?

3. Where are feelings or other factors preventing some members from functioning effectively and spontaneously? How free do persons feel to participate?

4. How is responsibility controlled and shared? Where does power lie in the group? How does the group respond to power figures and authority?

5. To what other persons and groups is this team related? What intergroup problems are anticipated or occurring?

6. How does the team make decisions? What factors aid or hinder decision making? Who influences whom? How are decisions implemented?

7. What kinds of member participation help the team? What kinds of participation prevent effective team task accomplishment?

8. How does the team deal with conflict? Is conflict denied, swept under the table, or faced and worked through?

9. How does the team gather data, both about members' feelings and about its task? Can the team develop more effective data gathering procedures to facilitate decision making?

10. How does the team clarify goals and make plans? Does the group recognize and deal with the detrimental effects of unclear task objectives? How does the team enter into both long-range and short-range planning?

Supervision should be seen as a privilege and as an opportunity to help another person grow and become more effective. Supervision really can be an exciting and fulfilling part of your ministry. Supervision allows you to affirm someone else even as you are affirmed.

4

Planning

One character in a novel is described as "getting on his horse and galloping off in all directions." Is it possible that an individual may be attempting to go in too many directions all at the same time? If that is the case, then the results are likely to be negative. Not only will there be severe stress for the person, but the intended destination, if one was intended, will probably not be reached. In a workshop on time management some clergy spoke of their fifty- or sixty-hour workweeks as the norm rather than the exception. Although they did not use the expression, some of the ministers seemed to feel that they were trying to "gallop in all directions." The frustration of these pastors was evident.

While ministry involves routine and repetition, there is also great variety. That variety can be exciting and challenging, but it can also be extremely time consuming. The expectations placed upon a minister and the tasks that need to be performed are enormous.

What is needed is a process of sorting it out. If a problem arises, analyze it and try to determine its components. Once the analysis has taken place begin to work on a solution. I believe that it was the philosopher William James who said that the first step in solving a problem is to state the problem clearly.

At the risk of generalization and oversimplification, let me state that for some clergy the inability to plan effectively and to organize is a serious problem. Without a clear sense of direction in their ministry, they find themselves galloping in too many different directions. They find it difficult to set priorities, often they do not manage their time well, and they do not accomplish what they would like to accomplish.

The Pastor's Role in the Planning Process

Earlier I emphasized the role of the pastor as leader and advocated a leadership style that was neither laissez faire nor authoritarian. Rather, the most desirable leadership style is a democratic style, a shared leadership style. If I were to suggest a model or image for this ministerial style of leadership, it would be that of the player-coach. The player-coach at times enters into the game itself, but at other times only coaches others who are playing the game. The coach has an assigned leadership role and is expected to bring special knowledge, experience, and skill to the players and to the playing of the game.

Another model or image or word that might describe the role of the minister is that of enabler. Pastors need to remember that one of the expectations placed on them is to be "equippers of the saints." The pastor is not only supported by the laity in her or his ministry but is also expected to support the laity in their ministry. Increasingly this understanding is being accepted, especially because in some congregations the work load is too much for one ordained minister. Yet finances or a shortage of clergy do not permit additional ordained or even paid staff. One description of the laity is that the laity are the *baptized ministers* of the church.

The pastor must be the visionary leader of the church. The pastor must be aware of possibilities for ministry that the laity have perhaps never thought much about or about which they are totally unaware. Yet the pastor must not assume that only her or his ideas are valid, or that her or his role is to convince the congregation to accept these ideas. Rather, the wise leader will utilize a shared planning process to encourage a mutual exchange of ideas and to develop a mission statement and objectives and goals for pastor and congregation.

Someone once remarked that "you can do a lot if you don't care who gets the credit." While it is tempting to want to get the credit for ideas that work and changes that are perceived as positive, the pastor needs to be willing to be the catalyst that starts the process for which other people ultimately get the credit. The role of the enabler is to help others to be leaders and to aid them and encourage them in their leadership.

Most local churches have an organizational structure of some kind in place. The structure may be specified or recommended by the denomination or it may have been worked out by the congregation. Whatever the case, the minister needs to learn quickly what the structure is and how it can best be utilized. The pastor needs to be clear about the role of the pastor in regard to the organizational structure of the congregation.

The kind of pastoral leadership that preceded the present pastor will impact the leadership expectations placed on the pastor by the congregation. If the laity of the congregation are accustomed to exercising their decision making authority with very little input from the pastor, the new pastor who is accustomed to an "I'm in charge" role may clash with the laity. Or if the congregation expects a pastor to provide strong active leadership and the pastor is accustomed to a more passive role in decision making, there will be tension as well.

Because of these possible differences, it becomes extremely important for the planning process to clarify the identity question. Clarification of role expectations and relationships must take place before constructive planning can occur.

A manual on managing a successful building program had this heading for one of its sections: "Take the congregation with you." A building committee should not get so far ahead in its planning and decision making that the larger congregation is in the dark about what is happening. "Don't get so far ahead that you get kicked from behind" is another bit of advice that an older, experienced pastor shared with me.

If the pastor enters wholeheartedly into this mutual planning process, the ministry of the laity will happen. Members will own the plans and commit to implementing those plans. The congregation will be kept informed of what is planned and members and friends of the congregation will be much more likely to participate.

The Planning Process

Although a church is not a business in the usual sense of that word, a church has some of the characteristics of a business. Perhaps we can learn something from the business world about planning and organizing. The concept of management by objectives (MBO) has become popular in business and industry. More recently the necessity of a team approach to manufacturing rather than a strictly hierarchical approach has been emphasized.

While the phrase "management by objectives" is not often used to describe what a local church is doing, more and more churches are doing precisely that. Churches are beginning to recognize the need for both short-term and long-range planning. While the process may vary, there are usually a series of steps that must be followed.

Below is a diagram that describes a planning process beginning with the group seeking to discover its identity and culminating in evaluation and celebration.[1] Notice that the diagram is in the form of a circle, indicating that the planning process is a continuing process. It is a never-ending process because as a group carries the process through to the evaluation stage, the group needs to reexamine its identity and purpose. The process itself and the passage of time bring about changes in personnel, in self-understanding, and very possibly in the purpose or mission of the organization. This requires a reenactment of the entire planning process

The Planning Process

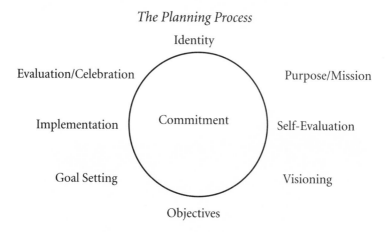

Identity

Evaluation/Celebration   Purpose/Mission

Implementation   Commitment   Self-Evaluation

Goal Setting   Visioning

Objectives

Mission Statement

The process may begin with a recommendation by the pastor that a small group of leaders work with the pastor to draft a purpose statement for the congregation. Sometimes this statement is called a mission statement. Usually the group spends some time reflecting on their identity as a community of faith. Questions are asked such as "Who are we? What has brought us together? What keeps us together? What are we called on to be? Why do we do what we do?" These questions ultimately lead to a fairly brief statement, perhaps only a paragraph or two, that states this congregation's understanding of its purpose. The statement is then presented for approval to a larger group of leaders and shared with the entire congregation.

Below is an actual statement of purpose adopted by a church in suburban Denver.

Purpose

In response to God's love, we the people of St. Andrew commit ourselves to a covenant relationship with God. We further commit ourselves to help all people come to a growing experience of the living Christ and the transforming power of the Holy Spirit. We will work to be a supportive, nurturing fellowship, thus enabling each person to respond in love, faith, and service within his/her community of influence.

Once the statement has been approved and shared, it becomes the basis for further self-evaluation. The purpose statement describes the ideal, what the church thinks it should be and wants to be. In all likelihood, however, this ideal has not been reached. Thus the congregation, and especially the pastor and leaders, must struggle with the gap between vision and reality.

Visioning

At some point in the planning process, the group can engage in what is often called brainstorming. This activity allows a group of people to share ideas or thoughts without any attempt to evaluate or prioritize them. The ideas are noted on newsprint or chalkboard, and later the group or a sub-group works with the many ideas presented. By not stopping to evaluate or prioritize, maximum creativity is attained. In this stage of thinking people are not allowed to criticize or raise objections to any thought expressed. That only comes later.

This time of brainstorming or free association can be exciting and can generate an amazing range of possibilities. People are usually told at this point in the process not to consider the cost of their idea or whether funds are available. These are dreams and visions of what could be. Of course, there must be awareness on the part of all persons involved that these ideas will need to be given much more thought and may or may not become accepted as objectives or goals for the organization.

Objectives

Out of this discussion can emerge possibilities of what positive things can be done to bring the vision into reality. At this point, the group tries to agree on some objectives. An objective is a general statement of intention for one aspect of the organization's purpose. For example, the purpose statement may refer to the importance of worship as the time when new possibilities for Christian living are emphasized. One of the objectives of the congregation, growing out of that purpose statement, might be to involve its members in regular attendance at worship.

Goals

The next step after stating the objective is to plan one or more goals (sometimes called action goals) that will help attain the objective. A goal is a statement of intention that specified people will act in specific ways by a specific time in the future, with observable and measurable results anticipated. The goal should answer these questions:
1. Who is to be involved?
2. What will they be doing?
3. What time table will they follow?
4. Why will they be doing this?
   (What is the basic purpose and/or desired outcome?)

Keeping in mind the objective stated above, an action goal might be: to begin to use attendance registration pads in the pews and to make telephone calls to members who are absent three consecutive Sundays. The goal statement would specify who is responsible for instituting the program, publicizing it, and making the phone calls. If callers need to be trained, then training needs to be planned. A timetable should be prepared, including times for evaluation and review. Expenditure of funds for registration pads may need to be authorized, even if the cost would be fairly minimal.

The SAM test can be applied to action goals.[2] The acronym stands for the words *specific, attainable,* and *measurable.* One of the differences between an objective and a goal is that the goal is *specific* about who will do what, by when, and with what results. These details need to be spelled out as part of the goal statement. If the *specifics* are not included in the initial statement, they should be added as soon as possible. In the process of trying to formulate specific details about how the goal is to be implemented, the group may discover that no one is willing to take the leadership role. Thus the goal is not realistic. If the specific details for implementation of the goal are not carefully considered in advance, the goal may never be accomplished. Goals need to be as specific as possible.

The goal needs to be attainable in the judgment of the people proposing it. We need to aim high when formulating a goal, not being overly pessimistic but at the same time being realistic. To set a totally unrealistic goal is to set up the group involved for discouragement and failure. For example, if the church is located in an area where the population is declining but the stated goal of the church is to double its membership in one year, there is little or no chance of success. Why not set a more realistic goal of a membership gain of 10 percent or 20 percent, assuming there are unchurched people in the community or friends of the church who may be persuaded to join the congregation?.

The third word in the SAM formula is *measurable*. One of the reasons for making the goal as specific as possible is that the goal then becomes measurable. This is particularly true of a quantitative goal. If the goal is to achieve a 10 percent net gain in membership in twelve months, at the end of twelve months it can readily be determined whether or not the goal has been attained. The more specific the wording of the goal statement, the more measurable the goal becomes.

Suppose the concern of the congregation is to encourage the spiritual growth of its members. That is really an objective rather than a goal. It then becomes necessary to decide upon some specific goals and methodologies by which that objective can be attained. Goals that might emerge could include such things as a new adult class on personal spiritual disciplines, the distribution of devotional booklets, more frequent observance of the Eucharist (Holy Communion), formation of neighborhood Bible study and prayer groups, a spiritual emphasis retreat, a series of sermons, and so forth. In each case the action goal related to the specific activity suggested would need to be spelled out in detail. Because the action goals are specific they become measurable, at least to some extent.

Implementation

If goals are to be implemented, the persons involved in the planning process must have a strong commitment. People must be willing to work if the goals of the congregation are to be attained. What we are really talking about here is commitment to Christ and to the mission of the church as defined in the purpose statement. Throughout this entire process participants must be genuinely and wholeheartedly committed. For the church this commitment is identified with Christ's commitment that led him to the cross. That is why the diagram of the planning process has the word *commitment* in the center. We in the church, as the present body of Christ, are called to full commitment. That is why the purpose or mission statement is so important. People need to be reminded *why* they are doing what they are doing.

Evaluation

Evaluation needs to be emphasized as an extremely important component of the planning process. While the word *evaluation* may be a negative one for some people, evaluation is a method of learning that needs to be utilized. It is done not to embarrass someone, but with an eye to the future. If the project failed, why did it fail? What could we have done differently, if anything, that would have resulted in success instead of failure? If the project was a success, what were the factors that made it successful? Even if it is judged to be a success, could anything have been done to make it an even greater success?

Evaluation, of course, needs to be ongoing, rather than reserved only for the end. Some process of monitoring, reviewing, and reporting should be determined before the project begins and should be built into the timetable. Feedback is a word that is sometimes used to describe this process of ongoing evaluation. In order to have helpful feedback, data must be gathered from persons involved in the project. Questionnaires, interviews, telephone calls, personal observation, as well as quantitative data (statistics), will help provide the necessary information for a thorough evaluation.

Celebration

If all has gone quite well and the action goal has been attained, some kind of recognition and celebration is appropriate. Recognition of persons involved (through notices in church bulletins or newsletters, or through public recognition in a worship service or other occasion) should be considered. Recognition can come before, during, and at the conclusion of a specific project.

The nature of the celebration will depend on a great many factors, including the nature of the goal, how many people were involved, how extensively they were involved, whether they want to celebrate in some way, and whether anyone will organize and implement the celebration. The celebration may be a brief time of sharing and a closing prayer at the conclusion of a meeting. It may be a potluck meal at someone's home, or recognition at a worship service or other church event.

The Minister's Personal Planning

Closely related to congregation planning is the minister's management of time. Many clergy seem to have problems managing time. There are good reasons for this. For one thing time management is seldom, if ever, taught in seminary. The topic may be touched on but noted only briefly in a class in church administration. At that point, the seminarian, with little or no actual experience in being the ministerial leader of a local church, does not fully appreciate the importance of the problem. In their educational experience, an instructor has provided a syllabus with topics designated for each day the class meets. Meeting times are predetermined and specific assignments are due on designated dates. Even the reading to be done for each class period may be noted.

Then the student begins the parish ministry, either as an intern or full-time pastor, and no longer is there an instructor to provide the syllabus. The neophyte pastor knows that there are certain scheduled events, such as worship services and board and committee meetings, but no one provides a schedule outlining how to spend the time each week. Initially, there seems to be considerable freedom to determine the schedule, but that freedom can be deceptive. Unless some serious planning and organizing takes place, the pastor may find that Sunday morning comes and he or she is still madly scribbling sermon notes to try to be ready for the worship service.

What kinds of time management problems can develop for the minister? Some of them are similar to those experienced by persons in other settings. Some are more unique to the minister.

Several years ago a survey was made of clergy to discover what the chief time-wasters were for them. Below are the "dirty dozen" the ministers said gave them the most trouble in managing their time. They are listed in order of importance, so that the first thing represents the largest amount of time wasted.[3]

1. Personal disorganization
2. Problems of delegation
3. Interruptions
4. Indecision and procrastination
5. Socializing
6. Junk mail and outside reading
7. Lack of planning

8. Television
9. Meetings
10. Family problems and family errands
11. Traveling time and car problems
12. Fatigue

This survey was conducted some years ago and represents a small sample of fifty clergy, all men. However, the responses do highlight some of the time management problems ministers encounter. The number one time-waster, personal disorganization, included "a lack of objectives" and "cluttered surroundings." These were lumped into one category because they indicated "a disorganized approach to the work situation."

The second most common problem, that of delegation, was twofold. Some ministers said they failed to delegate work they knew others could do. Other ministers stated they delegated little or no work because there were not enough capable people to whom the work could be delegated.

Two problems noted by ministers but not usually found in lists of business people were television and family problems. Because the minister has considerable freedom to plan his or her schedule, the minister may end up running family errands at times when the business person would be at the work place.

What can be done about these time-wasters? The same article suggested the DOE formula, stating that ministers need to delegate, organize, and eliminate.[4] Let's look at each of these possibilities.

Delegate

The minister must ask, What am I doing that someone else could be doing? In fact, if the minister thought about it for a while, the minister might think of someone who could do a particular task more efficiently than the minister and/or who might enjoy doing this task more than the minister does. The minister must learn to delegate whenever it is appropriate and possible.

For example, let's say the minister decides that the church should have a monthly newsletter mailed to all members and friends of the church. The minister presents the idea to the appropriate board or committee and gets approval of the idea and authorization to spend the money it will take to do this. Now the minister needs to decide who will do this. One option is for the minister to do this. The minister probably knows more about what is happening in the church than anyone else.

Let's assume the minister edited the college newspaper when a student and has good writing skills. Should the minister do this? My answer is, probably not. Even if the church has no paid secretary, there may be volunteers who could take on this project and would enjoy doing it.

Initially the pastor may need to spend more time training volunteers to do the newsletter than he or she would have spent doing it alone. But once the volunteers learn how to do the job, the opposite would be true. The minister needs to work with these people by providing some material for the newsletter and by encouraging them. However, the actual work will be done by the lay volunteers who will rightfully receive the grateful thanks of pastor and congregation.

Organize

We need to plan and to organize our time and not just our work. Most people do not really know how they actually use their time. It's important for the minister to find out how her or his time is actually used. The way to do this is to keep a log of how each day is spent during a week. The day can be blocked out in half-hour segments, beginning with wake-up time in the morning until bedtime at night. While each week will vary, this exercise in record keeping will provide information about how the minister's time is actually spent. Once this information is available, the minister can begin to plan and organize the use of time more efficiently.

One of the things we discover when we analyze our use of time is that we often spend too much time on things of lesser importance. Suppose your mail is delivered at about 10:30 A.M. to your church. Normally you set aside most of your mornings in your study or office (which term you use is significant) for sermon and worship preparation and perhaps some program planning. The mail comes to you in the midst of your sermon preparation and immediately your curiosity compels you to pick up the mail and sort it out. You read any personal letters and then the cover article in your denomination's clergy magazine catches your eye. Before you realize what is happening, you have picked up the magazine and started reading the article. Engrossed in your reading, you forget about the sermon preparation. Finally, you glance at your watch and are shocked that so much time has elapsed. There is no time to continue your sermon preparation, and even if there were time, you are no longer in the mood.

What could you have done differently? You could have put the mail aside until sermon preparation time was ended. Most of us have periods of the day when we are more efficient than at other times. For most people peak efficiency is in the morning, although some people through habit or because of their metabolism seem to possess more energy at other times. We need to schedule our time so that those tasks that are of greatest priority and perhaps most demanding are dealt with when we are most efficient and energetic.

Another way to organize is to list specific responsibilities for a specific period of time, whether a day, a week, or a month. Usually, of course, we would deal with one day at a time, although we would also list weekly and monthly tasks that need to be completed by a particular date and time.

The list of responsibilities needs to be prioritized, usually in three columns or categories. The headings might be:

A	B	C
High priority	*Medium priority*	*Low priority*
Must be done	Should be done if possible	Nice to get done but can wait

The problem is that the column C tasks are likely to be easier and more pleasant to do. The temptation then is to do them instead of confronting with all our energy the high priority tasks that may be more demanding and less enjoyable. However, organizing our responsibilities and prioritizing them with a list like this makes us aware of what needs to be done and which is most important. Thus the list itself becomes a motivator to get us working on the tasks.

When tasks seem unusually large, for example, visiting every member of the congregation, the minister becomes discouraged and never really gets started doing it. What needs to be done is to subdivide the task into manageable parts. Instead of thinking of the impossibility of visiting every member of a large congregation, the minister may want to determine which members most need a visit. Perhaps the priority would be persons unable to attend worship, such as shut-ins, persons in nursing homes and, of course, those persons in the hospital. Another priority might be members who are inactive but who still reside in the community.

Once the priority is established, the minister can determine a reasonable number of persons to be visited in a specified time, such as a week or a month. Now the task becomes possible and the minister can see a way to begin a huge task. The visitation can be organized by calling on all the members in a specific neighborhood. If the new pastor is unfamiliar with where people live in a large rural area, perhaps a retired parishioner can accompany the pastor and give travel directions so the minister does not waste time trying to figure out where someone lives. The possibility of delegating some of the calling may be a viable option, especially after the pastor has made the first call. Another option is to host a series of small informal gatherings of church members by neighborhoods, meeting in someone's home or in the pastor's home. The minister needs to be imaginative and intentional in planning how to best manage his or her time.

One other suggestion is to reward yourself in some way after you have carried out a significant task. Perhaps you can schedule some leisure time to enjoy a concert or a game of golf or even a short trip. Or perhaps a hot fudge sundae is your idea of a reward. Sometimes promising yourself a reward of some kind is a way to motivate yourself to action. If the satisfaction of simply getting the job done is sufficient, so be it.

Organizing time does pay off in greater efficiency. I have been told that if we were to take ten minutes at the end of the working day to organize the next day's activities, we would be at least 10 percent more efficient the next day.

Eliminate

The minister needs to ask, Is there anything I'm doing that does not need to be done at all? While some tasks can be delegated to others, some other tasks the minister is doing can be eliminated because they do not need to be done at all or are already being done by someone else or in some other way.

For example, suppose a small-town pastor has a post office box for church and personal mail, even though a carrier could deliver the mail directly to the church. The pastor may want to continue going to the post office each morning to pick up the mail because this enables the pastor to get some needed exercise, allows the pastor to meet and socialize with other people, and makes the mail available earlier in the day. However, if the pastor decided this daily walk to the post office was not important, the task could be eliminated.

Or to take another example, suppose the pastor is accustomed to writing out sermons in long hand, then typing the manuscript, and finally making brief notes to be taken into the pulpit. Could any of these steps be eliminated? Could the minister compose the sermon at a type-writer, or better still use a computer and word processor to prepare the sermon? Each pastor can think of other examples of how eliminating tasks can be another tool to achieve better management of time.

5

Reflecting

The pastor of a congregation surely is the resident theologian for that congregation. As the pastor leads worship, preaches, teaches, administers, and provides pastoral care, the pastor is trying to help people find meaning and direction in their lives. The pastor becomes an interpreter who links daily experience with religious faith. Surely the pastor is involved in pastoral theology, though the pastor's self-image may not be the same as that of the seminary professor of theology.

Professional is a good word and one that has often been applied to persons engaged in ministry. For some people, however, the word has a negative connotation. Perhaps when applied to the ordained minister, some think the word makes the ministry sound like a secular occupation rather than a sacred calling. In an article entitled "Ministry as Reflective Practice: A New Look at the Professional Model," Jackson W. Carroll identifies some of the criticisms leveled against the professional model of ministry:[1]

1. Creating a dependent laity. ("Holding up the clergy as experts who have a monopoly over important aspects of the church's life.")
2. A nontheological approach to ministry. (Theological education emphasizes particular bodies of knowledge and particular skills of ministry but "there is no theological core which enables a person to integrate the various elements, to bring together theology and practice into an integrated whole.")
3. Doing rather than being. ("The minister who has the skills but lacks spiritual depth.")

Carroll discusses each of these criticisms in depth and then goes on to rethink the professional model of ministry. He says that this rethinking must begin with ecclesiology and a consideration of the relationship of church and ministry. Carroll does not discount the need of the professional minister for specific competencies, but he believes that "expertise in theological reflection and envisioning is essential." He calls for clergy to be "reflective practitioners," which "includes the capacity . . . to analyze difficult and often novel situations and bring one's beliefs, commitments, knowledge and skills to bear in such a way that one's response is both appropriate to the situation and grounded in a sense of ministry."

Field education in some seminaries has been the primary means by which his concept of "reflective practitioner" has been introduced. While not claiming it is unique in doing so, field education has attempted to integrate theory, practice, doctrine, experience, action, and reflection. Both in student groups on campus and in on-site conferences between supervisor and student, theological reflection is encouraged. The orientation and training of supervisors includes an emphasis on the importance of theological reflection. By supporting field education in this manner, theological seminaries are attempting to prepare ministers to become comfortable and proficient in making theological reflection a part of their ministry.

Some Methods or Models of Theological Reflection

A number of methods or models of theological reflection have emerged in recent years. Among them are the tripolar model, the narrative model, and the four source model (sometimes described as the microscope method).

Tripolar Model

In *Method in Ministry* Evelyn and James Whitehead deal with the function of theological reflection in Christian ministry. They offer a helpful distinction between model and method, two words sometimes used interchangeably. "A model of theological reflection provides an image of the elements that are involved. . . . The method describes the dynamic or movement of the reflection." For the Whiteheads "theological reflection in ministry is the process by which a community of faith correlates the religious information from the sources of Christian tradition, personal experience, and culture in pursuit of information that will illumine and shape pastoral activity."[2]

There are three stages in the Whitehead method: attending, assertion, and decision. The first stage, *attending*, involves the posture of listening. In this stage the community seeks the information on a specific pastoral concern that is available from personal experience, Christian tradition, and cultural sources. When listening to these sources, it is important to suspend premature judgment or evaluation so there is a greater chance for new insight.

The second stage of theological reflection in the tripolar model is *assertion*. The concern of this stage is to "engage the information from the three sources in a process of mutual clarification and challenge in order to expand and deepen religious insight."[3] The two assumptions made in this stage are that God is revealed in all three sources and that each source reveals only partial information. Assertion is defined by the Whiteheads as "a style of behavior which acknowledges the value of my own needs and convictions in a manner that respects the needs and convictions of others."[4] The goal of this second stage of reflection is that a dialogue of mutual interpretation take place, leading to new insights and to the emergence of the shape of pastoral response.

The third stage in this model is *decision*, in which the community moves "from insight through decision to concrete pastoral action."[5] This stage attempts to take the insights developed in the earlier stages and derive from them a decision regarding appropriate ministerial action. The Whiteheads note a difference between theological reflection accountable only to academic theology, and ministerial reflection. That difference is that ministerial reflection usually focuses on a situation that has to be resolved in one way or another. As the Whiteheads put it, "the minister reflects in order to act."[6] This is not necessarily true of a theologian using theological reflection in an academic setting. The minister must sometimes act even when the information seems to be insufficient. The Whiteheads believe that this model of theological reflection can enable a minister and the community of faith to develop group consensus and to move from consensus to a plan for community action.

The Narrative Model

Another model of theological reflection that has recently come into prominence is the narrative model. Ken Pohly and Luke Smith have collaborated in research about "The Use of Narrative in Identity Formation: Implications for Supervision,"[7] and William R. Nelson has described a narrative model of theological reflection.[8]

There are some important parallels between the ideas of Pohly, Smith, and Nelson. Pohly and Smith focus on identity formation as one of the goals of the narrative model of theological reflection. Nelson stresses the importance of discovering one's "master story" as a paradigm for understanding oneself. He then uses these personal identity narratives as the focus for theological reflection. Pohly and Smith, in their discussion of identity formation, also call attention to the importance of listening for the "master story."[9]

Nelson defines theological reflection as "the interpretive exercise of reflecting upon God's story revealed in Scripture to test the self-concepts revealed in the events of daily life." He emphasizes the importance of the interaction between self and theological reflection. He says that "when subjected to theological reflection, our mundane stories can become the sacred stories which give meaning to our particular ministry."[10]

In his article, Nelson calls attention to a framework provided by Stanley Hauerwas for examining the theological implications of a master story. Hauerwas says that any story we adopt must display:

1. power to release us from destructive elements
2. ways of seeing through current distortions
3. room to keep us from having to resort to violence
4. a sense of the tragic and the way meaning transcends power[11]

In a seminar, Ken Pohly shared seven guidelines for using the narrative model of theological reflection:

1. enlarge the emerging story
2. recall the lived experiences
3. tap the received narrative
4. connect experience, narrative, and story
5. check for self-deception
6. "autobiograph" the story
7. explore the future

Tapping the received narrative could include consideration of tradition and the sacred. Pohly does not use the words "tradition" and "culture" when describing the model. Rather, he asks several probing questions under each of the guidelines.

During the seminar, Dr. Pohly led participants through an experience of theological reflection using the narrative model, and the guidelines seemed to work well. The sample supervisory incident was a problem that arose in connection with a church youth retreat. Use of the narrative generated a meaningful interchange of ideas and responses, culminating in our dealing with the implications of this particular reflection.

Four-Source Model (The Microscope Method)

Four categories can be used to sort out the ingredients of any life situation, problem, issue, or question. Together they form the four-source model, which provides "the framework for designing methods that connect life and faith and help people do theology in their everyday lives."[12] These four sources are

1. *Tradition* (This refers to Scripture, church history, stories of heroes and heroines, saints, doctrine, official church pronouncements, and the like. Tradition is the collection of the corporate memory of Christians, with each individual embodying a portion of the tradition.)

2. *Action* (Action contains all of what each of us does and experiences. Specific actions taken and the thoughts, feelings, and perspectives associated with the actions are included in this source. When constructing a spiritual autobiography, students in the seminar work primarily with this source.)

3. *Position* (This refers to the attitudes, opinions, beliefs, and convictions that a person holds.)

4. *Culture* (Culture includes the symbols, mores, assumptions, values, sciences, artifacts, and philosophies of human groupings. Culture also includes such formal disciplines of knowledge as literature, philosophy, psychology, music, and science.)

A simple outline of a deliberate reflection process might look like this:[13]

Experience:	*do* something
Identify:	*look* at what happened
Analyze:	*think* about meanings, interpretations, beliefs
Generalize:	*change* in understanding and/or action

The method of theological reflection derived from this four-source model is called the microscope method. It was developed by several persons at Bairnwick School of Theology, an Episcopal school, located on the campus of the University of the South in Sewanee, Tennessee. The method is used there in an ongoing weekly seminar, but it can be used in a single workshop as well. The originators of the method describe its purpose and context:

> The program presumes that through regular, committed, and communal reflection on life experiences, done in light of an increasing knowledge of the Christian Tradition, a person can be transformed; literally, that one can be formed into the mind and life of Christ, so that one can more clearly and consciously be a point of God's presence.[14]

The idea behind this method is that we can stop the flow of life long enough to look at a very small slice of life and learn from it what we can. In this method, a person in the group presents an incident or act of ministry upon which the group can focus in the same way that a researcher might look at a small slice of human tissue under a microscope.

In this microscope method the group members:

1. hear one member describe an act of ministry
2. list the decision points and choose one for reflection
3. listen to the presenter report on feelings and thoughts about the decision
4. describe when they have felt the same way
5. generalize these experiences in a metaphor
6. explore the perspectives contained in the metaphor
7. explore the world of tradition
8a. explore the world of our personal positions
8b. explore the world of cultural beliefs and assumptions
9. theologize (attempt to integrate our life experience with our understanding of God)
10. identify implications for action

A variation of the microscope method is called the issue method. This method focuses the reflection on an issue present in human experience rather than on an incident or act of ministry. The steps that are followed are essentially the same as in the microscope method.

Using Theological Reflection in Ministry

Because these models specify a structured process that takes time, the minister may decide not to do theological reflection in a formal way. I hope that is not the case because leading a group through this process can be very exciting. However, the important thing is for the pastor to accept the idea that theological reflection should be an important component of ministry and is something that can take place in different ways and at different times. The setting may be formal or informal, planned or spontaneous.

Each of these three models provides a fairly detailed process for doing theological reflection. In each case, following the process that is outlined requires a significant amount of time. While the process can be compressed and some steps dealt with lightly or perhaps even omitted, the results are better if more time is taken.

The pastor must often assume the role of interpreter, linking daily experience and religious faith through theological reflection. Here are some ways that theological reflection can be used as a tool in ministry:

1. *Peer support group.* Some clergy meet regularly (even weekly) with a small group of colleagues. These groups become a support community, even though they may focus on a task such as preparing to preach on a text from the common lectionary. Rather than having theological reflection take place on an occasional or unplanned basis, reflection can be structured into the agenda of the group. An individual pastor may need to take the initiative to organize such a group.

2. *Pastoral supervision.* As the pastor relates to other staff in a supervisory relationship, adding the dimension of theological reflection to the conversation can be helpful. Theological reflection need not always follow the extensive process outlined in the models described here but can give another perspective to a discussion. Sharing a significant incident or case study can be the starting point for an exciting time of theological reflection.

3. *Administration.* Theological reflection can be used in decision making to help a group move to consensus rather than being divided in a win/lose situation. The minister can help the various groups in the church place their business in the context of theological reflection.

4. *Pastoral care.* As people experience various crises in life they frequently ask "why" questions—"Why did this happen?" "Why me?" Those are theological questions, and when asked of the minister, open up the opportunity for theological reflection to take place.

5. *Worship and preaching.* As the worship service is planned and the sermon is prepared, the minister is surely engaged in theological reflection. How will the hymns that are sung, the Scripture that is read, the pastoral prayer that is spoken, the sermon that is preached relate religious faith to daily experience?

6. *Teaching.* How exciting it might be to offer a seminar in theological reflection, either on an ongoing basis or in a retreat format for interested persons in the congregation. The pastor can also train others to be leaders of a theological reflection group.

These are but a few ideas of how theological reflection might be more intentionally included in the life of the pastor and of the local church. Clergy in ministry settings other than a local church can also creatively utilize theological reflection and are urged to think of ways this could happen.

Implications of Theological Reflection for Field Education

Field education has been one of the ways theological reflection is made part of the curriculum of many theological seminaries. If indeed the task of the theological seminary is to prepare clergy who can function professionally as "reflective practitioners," as Jackson Carroll thinks they should, then theological reflection needs to occupy a more prominent place in a seminary curriculum. Theological reflection (in the sense of linking experience and faith) does take place in most of the courses taught in a theological school. Yet field education, because it is based on an action/reflection model, may be one of the best ways theological reflection can be introduced to persons preparing for ministry.

Pastors and congregations can participate in the preparation of persons for ministry by offering a field education placement in their parish for a seminary student. If the church is located too far away from a theological school to provide a part-time placement, perhaps a full-time internship can be arranged.

In most local church placements, the pastor (or one of the pastors, if there are more than one) serves as the supervisor. If given the privilege of supervising a seminary student, the pastor should plan to share in a process of theological reflection with the student. Theological reflection can be included in the weekly conference between supervisor and student. The student can include theological reflection in reporting on an experience of ministry, opening up the possibility of some very meaningful discussion.

Churches that have a field education student placed with them usually have a small committee of lay persons who meet regularly with the student. The committee is sometimes called the Teaching Church Committee or the Intern Committee. One of the ways the student and lay persons can use their time together is to engage in theological reflection around an act of ministry presented by the student. The student (or perhaps the supervising pastor) may need to take the initiative if this is to happen. Committees that have done this have found it to be an exciting and enlightening time of learning and sharing.

PART 2

Program Responsibilities

6

Administration

For some students and even for pastors in the field, administration is regarded as a negative aspect of ministry. Often it associated with words like boring, paper clips, problems, conflict, too much time, money, roof leaks, janitor quit, meetings, nothing done. However, administration, which is vital to ministry, can be a positive experience.

The word *administer* is derived from the Latin, *administrare,* meaning "to serve," coming from the same root as the word *minister.* This suggests that pastors of congregations must see administration as ministry. Administration is an expression of ministry rather than a barrier to ministry. Administration involves people more than it involves paper clips. Administration is a way of getting things done, a way of making things happen, a way of moving from point A to point B.

Administration is a way of clarifying the goals of the organization it serves and then moving toward their realization. In chapter 4 on planning we noted the importance of a church having a clear sense of purpose as expressed in a mission or purpose statement. The purpose statement helps the group determine its goals and objectives. Then the group has to determine by what means it will attempt to accomplish these goals. Implementation and evaluation follow. Administration includes all of these activities.

Church administration differs from business administration with respect to the objectives or aims of the organization. A business may have more than one aim, but usually the dominant one is to make a financial profit. Other aims may be to provide a useful product and to provide employment for a group of people. The church, on the other hand, is considered a not-for-profit organization. It is true, of course, that business organizations may end up being nonprofit, but that is not their intention. Likewise, some people related to the church are not clear about the aims and mission of the church. One pastor told me of his frustration with a church treasurer who tried to curtail the spending of the church in every way possible. This person wanted to measure the success of the church by how much money was unspent at the end of the year. The treasurer was confusing the aims of business with the aims of the church. The treasurer wanted the church to make a profit.

The Nature of the Church and Church Administration

Alvin J. Lindgren places church administration in the context of the nature and mission of the church. Lindgren summarizes the basic nature and mission of the church under three main headings:

1. The church as God's chosen community (the central concept of the Old Testament)
2. The church as the body of Christ (the most comprehensive and significant concept of the New Testament)
3. The church as a fellowship of redemptive love (a common mission of both concepts)

Lindgren discusses each of these images in detail, pointing out the implications for church administration. For example, when evaluating the goals of a present or proposed activity in the church, Lindgren says one of the questions that must be asked is, Are these goals in harmony with the nature and mission of the church?[1]

Lindgren offers a comprehensive definition of administration:

> Purposeful church administration is the involvement of the church in the discovery of her nature and mission and in moving in a coherent and comprehensive manner toward providing such experiences as will enable the church to utilize all her resources and personnel in the fulfillment of her mission in making known God's love for all people.[2]

Lindgren notes that his definition "involves all members of the church in administrative responsibilities," not just the pastor and a select few. Furthermore, Lindgren says that "purposeful church administration rests upon a God-centered, person-oriented polarity principle." God is the source and life of the church's mission. The ministry of the church is to persons. "Programs exist to serve persons and not persons to serve programs."[3]

Organizational Theories

Church administration is in some ways distinct from business or social administration, yet there is a body of knowledge underlying all areas of administrative study. This common element is usually referred to as organizational theory. An organization may be unaware of the specific theory that holds it together. However, an organization generally operates in one of five ways, which are reflected in five theories of management. While the names of these theories may vary, according to Peter Rudge the major organizational theories are:

1. Traditional—maintaining a tradition
2. Charismatic—pursuing an intuition
3. Classical—running a machine
4. Human relations—leading groups
5. Systemic—adapting a system[4]

The traditional theory describes an organization that has been in existence for some time and has a strong intention to continue to exist with as few changes as possible. Decision making is carried out in order to maintain the tradition. The leader of such an organization does not try to initiate new traditions but rather to embody and support the traditions already in existence.

The charismatic theory focuses on a charismatic leader who has some kind of intuition and then acts upon what he or she has perceived. The intuition may come as an inspiration or revelation that the leader then announces to all who will listen. Because of the personal charm or charisma of this person, people accept the content of the intuition and become followers of this charismatic leader. Decision making takes place as a kind of "instantaneous perception." The organization consists of the gathered people who look to their leader for continuing inspiration.

The classical theory sees the organization as a kind of machine formed in the shape of a pyramid. At the top of the pyramid is the leader who is expected to have the initiative and drive to keep the organization functioning smoothly. The objective is to maximize the efficiency of the machine. This theory is sometimes referred to as a bureaucratic organizational pattern.

The human relations theory places its emphasis upon leading groups. The organization is seen as a network of personal relationships within and between groups. These relationships are likely to be intimate and informal, as well as open to change. Even though there may be a number of groups within a larger organization, the members of each group focus more on their own group and thus are not likely to be aware of the wholeness of the organization.

People who are well educated, mature, and sensitive are likely to be the majority of persons involved in these groups. The initiative for planning and carrying out activities comes from the group. The leader needs to be a sensitive person who uses a permissive or nondirective style of leadership. Decision making takes place after people have been given an opportunity to express their feelings and when the group has come to a common mind.

The systemic theory is sometimes called the systems theory. It is a comprehensive approach to organizational development. A system is seen as a complete entity that consists of separate parts but is greater than the sum of all its parts. The structure and activities of the system are determined by the purpose for which the system exists and also by the environment in which the system is located. One of the chief characteristics of a system is that it is constantly adapting itself to the changes taking place in its environment.

The leader's role in the systemic approach to administration is to remind people of the purpose of the organization, to clarify continually that purpose, and to interpret the external changes taking place in the environment in which the organization is located. The leader's goal is to enable the whole system to respond to these changes in such a way that the purpose of the organization continues to be fulfilled.

Notice how differently the leader functions in each of the organizational patterns. Likewise the decision making process differs considerably in each theory. For example, in the classical theory the leader is the authority, and decisions are made and handed down from above. In contrast, the human relations theory assumes a fairly nondirective leader with decisions made as group members come to agreement, based on a shared understanding of the purpose of the group.

Peter F. Rudge relates each of these theories to various doctrines of the church and then suggests that the systemic (or systems) theory is most appropriate for church administration. In systems theory there is a strong focus on the ultimate objective or purpose of the organization. This ultimate purpose serves as a guide to determine whether specific actions should be taken. If we take Neibuhr's definition of the goal of the church as the "increase among (people) of the love of God and neighbor,"[5] then we have a clearly stated purpose to which our organization is committed.

Furthermore, the systems theory stresses the importance of the environment in which the organization is located. The organization needs to be aware of changes taking place in that environment and to be prepared to adapt itself to those changes. This ability to adapt and change is significantly different from the traditional organizational theory, which emphasizes maintaining the status quo.[6]

The Role of the Pastor

Regardless of which organizational theory is in use, the pastor is a key to what happens in the life of the congregation. In earlier chapters we have noted certain characteristics and skills that a minister must embody in order to be effective. The pastor needs to care about people, be a leader, and know how to communicate, plan, supervise, and reflect. When thinking about the pastor as administrator, we may also want to add the word *manage* to this list.

Interestingly the biblical roles of the minister have sometimes been identified as prophet, priest, and pastor. Administrator or manager do not appear in this list. However, John Calvin, in his *Institutes*, suggests that the traditional images or tasks of the minister are prophetic, priestly, and kingly. The kingly role suggests the administrative or managerial task of the minister. The United Methodist Church ordains its clergy to "Word, Sacrament and Order." There is a kind of dual interpretation given to the word "order." In one sense it seems to refer to the rite of ordination, but it can also be understood as referring to maintaining the order or organization of the church.

Alvin J. Lindgren and Norman Shawchuck suggest three main tasks of the pastor as church manager. These are

1. to clarify the specific purpose and mission of the church,
2. to involve persons in ways that will facilitate mission and promote personal growth, and
3. to consider the social impacts and responsibilities of church actions.[7]

These are broadly stated tasks and, of course, the minister's work of administration deals with much more specific areas of concern.

Administrative Areas

Several administrative areas are interrelated yet can be looked at separately: (1) program, (2) record keeping, (3) buildings and grounds, and
(4) finance. Another major area relates to the other people involved in
the work of ministry in the church. We will give special attention to
sharing ministry with the laity in the last part of this chapter. Each of
these areas can be considered part of the general administrative responsibility of the minister.

Program

Unless someone is part of a minister's family, is an employee of the
church, or has an active leadership role, he or she has little awareness of
the activities and responsibilities that lay claim to a minister's time. You
may want to list all the activities that go on in the church or that the
church sponsors, and then ask, What is the pastor's role in relationship
to this myriad of activities? The pastor must be clear about the nature
and mission of the church, then prioritize and manage the time available for ministry. Some suggestions about how to do this were mentioned in chapter 4, "Planning."

One of the frustrations of the pastor is that there never seems to be
enough time to do all that needs to be done. A second frustration may
be the difficulty of communicating within the organizational structures
of the church. One way to begin to deal with these two problems is to
schedule an annual planning retreat for church leaders. Preferably this
retreat should be at a location other than the local church and
overnight, perhaps beginning with the evening meal on Friday and concluding late afternoon on Saturday. By getting away from their own
church, the people are less likely to be pulled away from the retreat
because of local responsibilities. By staying together for a more extended time, including several meals, some good fellowship can take place.
Also, there is more time for planning and communication.

Developing a mission or purpose statement should be one of the
tasks of the retreat. If the congregation has such a statement, it can be
reviewed to see if it still expresses the intention of the congregation. The
statement can be used as a guide by which to measure the activities of
the congregation and to stimulate thinking about new possibilities.
Some free wheeling brainstorming can be fun and productive when
developing program possibilities.

A simple threefold process of evaluating the various groups and activities of the church, in addition to using the mission-purpose statement, involves these questions.

1. What are we doing that is going well and should be continued?
2. What are we doing that is not going as well as it should? How can we make it better? Or should it be discontinued?
3. What are we not doing that we should be doing?

Depending upon the answers to these questions, the group can begin the more extensive planning process suggested in chapter 4.

Another problem for the pastor (and for some of the lay people as well) is the multiplicity of meetings. Some churches find it helpful to schedule a designated evening as committee night. Often the group meets for a simple meal, moves into committee time, and then reconvenes to share decisions made and to secure group approval, if that is needed. The pastor is available for consultation throughout the evening.

Keeping a master calendar and making certain that nothing is put on it without the approval of the person in charge can prevent potential conflict over use of time and space. Having available printed, agreed-upon policy information about such matters as weddings, funerals, and the use of the building by outside groups can be helpful to the pastor, who is often the spokesperson for the church.

Record Keeping

Record keeping is another aspect of church administration that needs to be emphasized. Churches and pastors are often negligent in this important area. Some pastors see it as an unpleasant, time consuming, and perhaps even unnecessary task. Yet the pastor is the one ultimately responsible for keeping good records, even though the actual task may be delegated to a secretary or conscientious volunteer. Even then the pastor must see that this person promptly receives accurate information to be recorded.

Records kept in a systematic fashion provide the pastor with a wealth of clues for pastoral care. Such records provide the statistical information for annual reports to the congregation and the denomination. Some religious occasions have legal significance. Baptismal records may be used to establish age for retirement or to obtain a passport. Accurate marriage and death records could be a factor in litigation.

Early in the first pastorate is the time to develop an accurate record keeping system and to develop the habit of entering data when it occurs. That means that you go back to your church office after the wedding and enter the requisite data in your church and personal records. You do this before you mail the license back to the county clerk and before you become occupied with other tasks. Keeping accurate records only requires a few minutes a week. Reconstructing unkept records wastes many hours. Not only will you benefit greatly by keeping good records, the pastor who follows you will be extremely grateful.

Buildings and Grounds

The maintenance of facilities and grounds is usually not included in a pastor's job description. There must be only a few pastors, however, who have not found it necessary to take direct personal action in response to an immediate need. This is more likely to happen in a smaller congregation that makes less frequent use of its facilities and depends primarily on volunteers.

However, in any congregation, regardless of size, a designated group should oversee the care and use of buildings. Such a group is sometimes designated as the board of trustees and is usually the legal entity that acts on behalf of the congregation regarding real estate matters, insurance, and use of the building. The pastor is normally an ex-officio member of the board of trustees and should maintain a cordial, open relationship with its members.

Communication is extremely important in regard to the work of the trustees. The programs of the church affect the use of the building, and the policies of the board regarding the use of the building directly impact the programs. The use of the building by outside groups needs to be carefully considered and a policy agreed upon. The pastor should assist in preparing that policy statement and appreciate the fact that a stated policy makes the pastor's task easier. The pastor is often the one contacted by outside groups and can get into serious difficulty if he or she makes decisions unilaterally.

When determining the policy regarding building use, the systems theory of organization is useful. The church's purpose needs to be remembered, at the same time the needs of the environment (community) in which the church is located must be considered. The need for the church to change its policies and programs as the community environment changes must also be recognized. The pastor as leader needs to maintain contact with the trustees and the other decision making and program groups in the church. The pastor needs to help clarify the purpose of the church and interpret the changing needs of the environment. The role of interpreter is an extremely significant aspect of pastoral leadership.

Finance

Most churches have a financial secretary who keeps the records of giving to the church. In addition, a church treasurer works with the budget and pays the bills. Sometimes the same person does both. These persons need to be carefully chosen because their positions require some special skills, including a high degree of honesty.

Fund raising is essential if the church is to survive and carry out its mission. Most churches request their members to make an annual pledge or (to use a term some persons prefer) make an estimate of giving. (These are not binding financial obligations and can be changed.) Each church has to figure out how its stewardship and finance program can best be carried out. In some rural areas where farmers and ranchers do not have a regular weekly or monthly income, the gifts to the church will be made as larger sums on an occasional basis. The work of stewardship education and implementation needs to be carried out by a competent committee in consultation with the pastor. While the pastor may preach on stewardship, the appeal to the congregation for financial support should be given by lay people.

The church must make certain that there is no suspicion of improper handling of funds. In larger churches, persons who handle the funds of the church are often bonded. Even if bonded, several persons as a team should count the Sunday offering before the money leaves the church. All financial records need to be audited, perhaps in a small church by a volunteer person or committee. The financial work of the church needs to be handled in a totally businesslike manner.

Computers make this financial task much easier than it once was, and a number of churches do much of their record keeping on computers. In addition to keeping financial records and statistics, the computer can serve other useful purposes, such as keeping membership records, mailing lists, and attendance figures. The advantage of a computer over a book or card filing system is that the computer can provide rapid access to information, can easily be used to update information and organize the information as needed.

When a church has a computer, the word processing facility can be used in a number of ways. The pastor's sermons, worship bulletins, various reports, the church newsletter, and form letters to members are appropriate projects for a computer.

A well-equipped church office is essential to making efficient use of time. In addition to computers, churches are making good use of copiers, dictaphone equipment, and telephone services like voice mail or an answering machine. More devices to make the administrative work of the church easier and quicker can surely be expected to become available.

Sharing Ministry with the Laity

A strong church has many people involved in leadership. There is no way the pastor can function effectively without the support and help of the laity. Our ministry is a mutual ministry in which we are supportive of one another. Some ministers are ordained as well as baptized, but all baptized Christians are baptized ministers.

Larger congregations often employ lay persons in ministry positions. Such persons may direct the Christian education or youth program of the church. They may be in charge of a church-operated day care center. Others may be responsible for a visitation program, especially to shut-ins. They may be the administrator for the church or do counseling. They may direct the music program or serve as organist. The work of the custodian can also be seen as ministry.

In addition to the paid lay professionals, many other persons serve as volunteers for the church. The list of activities carried out by volunteers, even in a relatively small church, is a long list, far too long to enumerate here.

Acts 6 describes how the early Christian church responded to the problem of an increasing need for people to share in ministry. The church was increasing in number (Acts 6:1). Some of these new converts were Hebrew Jews and some were Hellenists (Greek speaking Jews or Jews who had adopted Greek customs). Apparently the church provided a daily distribution of food to widows, and "the Hellenists murmured against the Hebrews because their widows were neglected in the daily distribution" (Acts 6:1).

The clergy leadership (the twelve apostles) initiated a process to share their ministry with the laity. It involved these steps:

1. *Need recognized.* The problem is clearly stated, namely that the Hellenist widows were being neglected in the daily food distribu-

tion. The Hellenists did not keep quiet about this. They spoke up and their complaint was heard. Each church needs to ask, "Where and how in our church can criticisms be made and negative feelings expressed? How do we allow for that to happen? Or do we try to stifle criticism and tell complainers to be quiet?

2. *Plan proposed.* The twelve leaders took the complaint seriously. No doubt they investigated and found the complaint to be true. They then devised a plan to present to the larger body. They did not use their authority in a dictatorial way. Leaders do have authority but are wise if they use that authority in a consultative way. They can do some strategic planning and then present their proposal to the larger group for consideration. This incident in Acts is an example of the democratic or shared leadership style recommended in chapter 3, "Leading and Supervising."

3. *Plan accepted.* Apparently without hesitation the community accepted the plan proposed by the Twelve. By letting the people discuss the plan and then accept it, the Twelve enabled the people to take ownership of the plan so they became committed to its implementation.

4. *People chosen.* The Twelve recommended that seven men be chosen for this task and listed three specific criteria by which these men should be chosen. They were to be men "of good repute, full of the Spirit and of wisdom" (Acts 6:5). Sometimes in the church today we are so eager to fill a position that we do not adequately consider the qualifications needed in the person being invited to serve. The church needs to use criteria like those used in Acts in determining the qualifications of persons for leadership in the church.

5. *Recognition given.* The selection of the seven was an event considered important enough to be recorded in Acts. This must have been an impressive occasion, especially for those who were chosen for this special ministry of service. They were commissioned through prayer and the laying on of hands. Are people commissioned or installed into leadership positions today in a way that says to the person being installed, You have been chosen to do something important? Are those seated in the congregation called upon to pledge their support of the persons who have accepted leadership responsibility?

6. *Program evaluated.* There is no mention in Acts of any formal

process of evaluation of this program and its new leadership, but according to Acts 6:7 the results were extremely positive. The importance of monitoring a program and evaluating its effectiveness needs to be stressed. Too often evaluation is seen only as something negative and thus is avoided. People need to realize that affirmation is a part of evaluation. When the evaluation is positive, a time of celebration is appropriate. Churches need to say "thank you" to people who accept responsibility and carry it out well. Churches need to celebrate accomplishments.

Just as the apostles realized that they alone could not do all that needed to be done, so the clergy of today must recognize that they too need to share their ministry with the laity.

Volunteers Wanted

In spite of the large number of volunteers serving in churches, pastors are finding it increasingly difficult to get people to accept church leadership positions. There are some demographic reasons why volunteers are more difficult for the church to secure even though they may be more needed than ever before. In the baby boomer generation, persons born between 1946 and 1964, 70 percent of the women work outside the home. Thus a large number of persons who previously were potential volunteers is no longer available.

The competition for volunteers is increasing. Many agencies and institutions are seeking volunteers. Schools, hospitals, prisons, service clubs, drama and music groups are but a few of the places where volunteers are needed. Most people employed outside the home jealously guard their leisure time. If they volunteer at all, it will be on a limited basis and usually for only one institution or cause.

The potential for finding volunteers is probably greater among teenagers and senior citizens than any other age group. According to Marlene Wilson, a noted authority on volunteers, high school students contribute about seventeen million hours of volunteer work annually. College students contribute 192 million hours.[8] Young people are trying to find meaning for their lives and if properly challenged will respond strongly to an obvious need. They can be helped to realize they need volunteer experience. These young people have a high energy level and bring enthusiasm to their volunteering.

Actually there are more people in this country over sixty-five, about thirty million as of 1990, than there are teens. This age group is the most rapidly growing population group.[9] While some may have limitations because of health and stamina, seniors make great volunteers. They have time. They are dependable. They have a lot of life experience, which should result in some wisdom. A volunteer position may bring new meaning into their lives. It may give them a purpose for living, something to anticipate, something that may give them a sense of recognition and importance.

Why Do People Volunteer?

Perhaps if we are aware of the factors that motivate people to volunteer we will be more successful in securing volunteers. A person may accept a volunteer position for selfish as well as altruistic reasons. Being involved in an activity or duty has to have some payback for the person, or the individual is not likely to continue doing it. People have many reasons for volunteering.

1. *They recognize a need is important.* When a person is recruited for leadership in the church, he or she needs to believe a real need exists. Saying to a prospective volunteer "We just need to write in a name so that the denomination knows where to send mail" is not a convincing need.

2. *They are asked.* Sometimes a person will recognize a need in the church and volunteer to fill it. Such a request is an exception rather than the rule. In most cases, people need to be asked to assume a position. Who does the asking and how the person is asked can make a big difference in the response.

3. *They believe the task is something they can do.* Many skills are transferable from one setting to another. The attitude of a person is tremendously important. If the person being asked is excited about the opportunity and eager to learn how to do the job effectively, there is a strong probability the experience will be a positive one.

4. *They have had a previous positive volunteer experience.* An individual's previous experience as a volunteer will affect that person's attitude toward future volunteer opportunities. If the prior experience has been negative, the answer to a new request is likely to be no. If that is the case, it would be important to find out what went wrong and see what the disillusioned volunteer and the person extending the invitation might learn from the experience. If the prior experience has been positive, the volunteer and recruiter

might try to determine what made it positive. Again, some important learning can take place.

5. *They feel needed and wanted.* Being asked to do something important in the life of the church or for the community is flattering. The need for belonging is a significant need, and when we are asked to assume a responsibility, there is a sense in which we are being assured that we belong.

6. *They see this opportunity as an expression of Christian ministry.* Numerous scripture passages suggest that Christians are called to love and serve others. Jesus said that the first commandment is to love God with all your heart, soul, and mind, and the second commandment is to love your neighbor as yourself (Matthew 22:37-39). When asking lay people to accept responsibility for the program and outreach needs of the church, we should clearly state that such service is a fulfillment of our ministry. What we do for others we do for Christ.

7. *They find satisfaction in helping others.* To know we have made a positive difference in the life of another person can be a great source of satisfaction. There is no monetary compensation but we feel good when we know we have done something constructive, something that has helped someone. The gratitude of the person who has been helped is adequate compensation, say many volunteers.

8. *They meet interesting persons.* For example, in Denver, volunteers carry on the work of the Widowed Persons Service. These volunteers telephone and visit newly widowed persons and assist them in dealing with the grief and the practical problems related to the death of a spouse. Regular programs and fellowship opportunities are provided by Widowed Persons Service for any interested widowed persons. These volunteers have found a way to deal with their own grief and loneliness by reaching out to others. They meet new people and make new friends.

9. *They have time.* Retired people obviously have more time available for volunteer work than younger people who are employed outside the home or who have young children for whom they are responsible. An increasing number of people are taking early retirement, and they have the energy and desire to be involved in some activity. Many of these persons have excellent professional or technical skills that can be put to good use. Although

retirees as a group are often seen as the most available volunteers, the church should not overlook younger employed persons as well. Even busy people will somehow find time for something they consider important. Do not write off prospects for
church positions because *you* think they are too busy. Let them
decide if they are too busy or if they are willing to reconsider
their priorities.

Strengthening a Lay Ministries Program

Using some of the ideas from chapter 4 on planning, let's see how a
local church can strengthen the involvement of lay people in ministry.
An ad hoc committee or task force can begin the process or an existing
group can be given the responsibility.

1. *Develop a mission statement.* The mission statement is a means of
getting agreement and ownership about what the church should be
doing. The mission statement then leads to specific objectives and
action goals. These action goals require a plan by which each goal can
be implemented and its attainment measured. The jobs people are
asked to do need to tie in with the mission statement.

For example, in a newly formed congregation, the needs for funds
was great. A woman who attended worship but who was not a member
suggested the church arrange to buy a new car and then sell raffle tickets
for the car. She was disappointed when the pastor explained that such a
plan was not in keeping with the social principles of the denomination
to which the congregation belonged. In effect, the mission statement of
the denomination ruled out this particular fund-raising activity.

If the church already has a mission statement, the statement should
be evaluated by asking, Does the statement reflect the present missional
intentions of the congregation? Is there anything in the statement that
should be deleted? Is anything missing in the statement that should be
added? How well is the church fulfilling its mission?

2. *Identify areas of need not adequately addressed or staffed.* The
preparation or review of the mission statement will likely suggest areas
of need that are not being addressed at all or that are being dealt with
inadequately. The committee or board in the church doing this review
should determine why a specific need is not being adequately met.

Suppose the church previously identified a need for nursery care
during the worship service. However, few parents are bringing their
children to the nursery. There could be a number of reasons this is hap-

pening—some people are unaware the nursery exists, some people prefer to keep their children with them in worship, the nursery is not attractive and/or not kept clean, or perhaps the staffing of the nursery is inadequate.

Once the problem is diagnosed, the investigating group can suggest possible solutions, such as better publicity about the nursery, redecorating and purchasing new equipment, systematically staffing the nursery through a coordinator of volunteers, and establishing a list of back-up persons to cover if someone cannot be there.

3. *Build a talent bank.* Annually a church should ask its members to complete or update a talent questionnaire. This will provide the church with names of people with specific skills who are willing to serve the church in some capacity. This information can be put into a computer and then retrieved when a specific need develops. Changes can also be easily made.

Be sure to acknowledge each person's response and let the person know if he or she is needed for a specific task. If people indicate their willingness to be involved in some way and then hear nothing more, they will become frustrated. At the very least, extend the courtesy of saying "thank you" and letting the person know he or she will be contacted if needed.

The talent questionnaire is a useful tool, but the pastor and lay leaders of the congregation should also be asking people one-on-one what they like to do. Instead of starting with slots to be filled, a church can also work hard at finding slots for talented people to fill.

4. *Prepare job descriptions and time lines.* The program or task for which help is needed may be an existing one, in which case the need is for a replacement volunteer, or it may be new, arising out of an unmet need that has been identified. In either case, a job description needs to be prepared. A preliminary time line should be constructed as well, so the process moves according to schedule.

If the job description is accurate and realistic, a better match of job and person can take place. Do not describe the position as less or more than it really is. Job descriptions can be revised, of course, when experience shows this is necessary. The time line provides information to the volunteer about the length of commitment to be expected. It is a mistake to ask people to serve for some indefinite length of time. Asking for a shorter specific commitment allows the person to exit from the position without being embarrassed. Likewise, when the commitment time ends, the church has the option of replacing the person or asking the person to continue.

5. *Make leadership training available.* Periodically the church should provide training opportunities in such areas as public speaking, leadership skills, conducting a meeting, teaching a class, the structure of the church, or evangelism. The local church can subsidize the cost of people attending training events away from their own church. Ecumenical as well as denominational educational opportunities should be brought to the attention of local church members, and they should be encouraged to attend. Try to get new people, not just those already in leadership roles, to attend these events. In this way you expand your cadre of trained personnel.

6. *Gently move ineffective people out of leadership.* People sometimes stay in a position too long. They become accustomed to doing something one way and only that way. They resist any suggested change. Also, people in the wrong slot may not realize they are in the wrong slot. Some people simply do not do the job they promised to do when they accepted a leadership role in the church. Such a person needs to be dealt with in face-to-face conversation to determine why this is happening. Perhaps the person is angry about some real or imagined slight. Maybe demands of family and work do not allow time for church leadership. A feeling of inadequacy may cause the person to withdraw. Whatever the cause of the problem, once it is acknowledged it can be dealt with in as helpful a way as possible. The person may even be relieved to be offered the chance to resign and let someone else take over. Term limitations are a good way to avoid such problems. Leadership is rotated and people are not offended when their term ends and someone else takes over. If absolutely necessary in a small church or in regard to a position that requires unusual skills, an exception can be made to the term limitation rule.

7. *Give ongoing support and recognition.* The lay ministry program should be structured in such a way that accountability is clear. Accountability allows monitoring to take place. This means that a potential problem can be discussed and resolved before it becomes a major problem. Fellowship times need to be built into the schedule. Publicity in the church bulletin or newsletter provides affirmation and recognition. And a sincere word of commendation will be much appreciated.

Effective Church Administration

We have seen that administration is an essential component of effective ministry and that the pastor has a key role in leading the church as an organization. Regardless of how the church is organized, it is useful to review some essential characteristics of effective church administration.

1. *Shared sense of vision and purpose.* The nature and mission of the church needs to provide the context for determining what the church should be doing. Each congregation has to figure out what that means for its particular place and time.

2. *Mutual consideration and respect between clergy and laity.* Pastor and people need each other. The biblical image of the church as the body of Christ comes to mind as the relevant image when we think of the church as an organization.

3. *Participatory decision making.* While the pastor is the designated leader of the church, the pastor should not be the dictator who makes unilateral decisions and then issues decrees the ordinary church members are expected to obey. Rather, the pastor needs to operate in a democratic way that allows for discussion and input, leading to ownership and commitment by laity and pastor to the decisions.

4. *Clear communication.* An organization needs to check continually on its internal and external communications. Much of the conflict that develops in any organization could be avoided if clear and timely communication took place. "Keep the congregation informed" should be the motto for any leader or group in the church. Likewise, most churches could do a much better job of external communication. Good public relations should be considered a necessity, not an option.

5. *Awareness of its environment.* One of the strengths of the systems theory of organizational development is its emphasis on relating to the environment in which the organization is related. The church needs to be aware of the persons, groups, agencies, institutions, and businesses that make up its immediate neighborhood and larger community. Cooperation may be possible rather than conflict. The church can help shape its environment, as well as be shaped by it.

In this chapter we have talked about the transformation process that can take place through use of a systems approach to church administration. The input that the church receives is transformed into output. Don S. Browning in his comprehensive and challenging book, *A Fundamental Practical Theology*, says:

> In my view transformation follows the dynamics of dialogue in a practice-theory-practice rhythm. Because it is dialogical, the transformative process is mutual. From a Christian theological perspective, God is always finally the agent of transformation. All other agents of transformation—community, minister, lay leader—are metaphors of God's deeper transformative love.[10]

Browning reminds us that God does the transforming and we are God's agents in the transforming process. Church administration helps enable that transforming process to take place.

7

Pastoral Care

Pastor John Adams is ready to begin his evening meal with his family when the telephone rings. The wife of the president of the Board of Trustees is calling: "I'm sorry to bother you at home, but I'm at the hospital. Bill was just brought in by ambulance. I think he's had a heart attack. I thought you would want to know. Maybe you could stop by and see him this evening."

Pastor Adams replies, "I'm so sorry to hear that, Marge, and I'm glad you called to let me know. Of course, I'll stop by. I was just ready to eat supper when you called so I'll take time to eat a quick bite and then be over there. That should give the doctors a little time to work with him without interruption, which I'm sure they need to do."

"Thank you so much. I'll see you soon," says Marge.

Pastor Adams explains to his family what has happened and then sits down to a meal that he does not enjoy as much as he had anticipated. He hurries through the meal, thinking that perhaps he should have gone to the hospital immediately. Skipping dessert, he leaves for the hospital, knowing that he has a worship committee meeting to attend later that evening.

Such is life for the parish pastor. There is almost always someone in the parish who is experiencing a need, although those needs sometimes surface quickly and unexpectedly. The conscientious and caring pastor seeks to respond to those needs even though that response may interrupt other plans.

While often pastoral care is required in response to a crisis, at other times pastoral care may take the form of consultation and guidance. The term *pastoral care* may imply that such care is solely the responsibility of the pastor. Although the pastor may be seen as the primary caregiver in the congregation, it would be a mistake to think of the pastor as the only caregiver. The members and friends of the congregation are involved in pastoral care as well.

In the case of the man taken to the hospital with an apparent heart attack, Pastor Adams likely shared that news with the worship committee at the meeting he attended later that evening. As soon as members of the congregation learned what happened, they probably sent cards and flowers. If visitors were permitted, other people in addition to the pastor would call on Bill. Some people might bring food to Marge or invite her to have a meal with them. Bill and Marge would be remembered in prayer by friends in the congregation. At Sunday morning worship or other times church members are together, prayers would be offered for Bill and Marge. If Bill were to die from the heart attack, a whole new range of pastoral care would be forthcoming from the pastor and the congregation.

Pastoral Care and Counseling

The words pastoral care and counseling are often linked, as though they refer to one activity. While this may sometimes be the case, it is helpful to make a distinction between pastoral care and pastoral counseling. Pastoral care should be seen as a broader, more comprehensive ministry than the traditional counseling relationship in which one person counsels another. All pastoral counseling is a form of pastoral care, but not all pastoral care involves counseling. For example, the worship life of the congregation may be seen as a form of pastoral care, but it is quite different from a counseling session in the pastor's study. We would not refer to the counseling session as a worship experience.

Regardless of how we define these terms, people still turn to a minister, priest, or rabbi with a great variety of needs or problems. Sometimes the problems are spiritual, and the pastor may take on the role of spiritual guide or director. Someone who is unemployed may seek the minister's help in finding a job. Marital discord, spousal abuse, or child abuse may cause someone to turn to the minister for guidance and help. Likewise, someone with a substance addiction problem (be it alcohol or drugs) may turn to a minister, priest, or rabbi for help.

The Pastor as Counselor

Every pastor should expect to be involved in both pastoral care and pastoral counseling. The key question is, how much should the pastor be involved, particularly in pastoral counseling.

Some large congregations now have a designated minister of counseling who is specially trained to do extended counseling. Sometimes a fee is expected or required, but the fee is usually adjusted according to the financial situation of the counselee. Even though another minister of the congregation may be the first one contacted by an individual in need, the person is usually referred to the minister of counseling, especially if extended counseling seems necessary or likely.

Another arrangement that is becoming more common is for a group of congregations to establish a pastoral counseling center, either in one of the church buildings or in another location. Such an arrangement reduces the cost to any one church. The counseling services are available to anyone, but members of participating congregations can receive counseling at a reduced rate. They may also be given priority in scheduling appointments.

Hospitals and other institutions related to a religious organization, theological seminaries, and even individual clergy with specialized training may also offer pastoral counseling services to the public. Of course, there are numerous other counseling centers, agencies, and institutions, especially in urban areas, that provide counseling that is not specifically pastoral or religious. Various governmental agencies at the local, county, state, and federal level also offer counseling.

The pastor needs to become well-informed of these other resources so he or she can provide information and make referrals. However, the question remains to what extent the pastor personally should become involved in counseling. Each minister needs to make that determination in consultation with the lay leadership of the congregation. Some questions the pastor needs to ask in order to arrive at a decision include:

1. What training do I have that prepares and qualifies me for counseling? Many pastors really do not have the specialized training and experience that qualifies them to deal with the complex problems that may be presented to them.

2. How much time can I (should I) give to individual counseling? The demands of pastoral ministry are many and varied. Counseling an individual or couple over an extended period can take a large amount of time. Is this the best use of the minister's time?

3. What other counseling resources are available in this community or nearby? Ministers may wish to do some initial counseling (a kind of screening process) and then make a referral if it appears that extended counseling (more than three or four sessions) will be needed.

4. What importance does my congregation place on my role as a pastoral counselor in relationship to my other responsibilities? The pastor needs to discuss with the appropriate group, such as the pastor-parish relations committee, the various responsibilities the pastor has and the time involved. This committee can help the pastor prioritize duties.

5. Can I maintain the confidentiality of a counseling relationship? Confidentiality is a must for any counselor.

6. Can I be involved in an extended counseling relationship without becoming emotionally involved in an inappropriate way with the counselee? Unfortuantely, problems of sexual involvement may develop in an ongoing relationship in which the counselor (the person of trust) fails to maintain the professional relationship.

7. Should I limit my counseling to members and friends of the congregation? Because of time limitations, some ministers use this as a helpful guideline but not an absolute rule. Others encourage nonmembers to come for counseling, seeing this as a service the church renders to the community, as well as a way to introduce persons to the church.

8. Are there persons within my congregation who could assist me and supplement the counseling I am asked to do? There may be people with special knowledge and skills who would be willing to share the counseling load. Such persons might include attorneys, physicians, school or vocational counselors who are retired or who would volunteer a few hours weekly.

9. Could a support group or educational program be offered by the church (or several churches) to meet some of the needs that must otherwise be dealt with on an individual basis? Some churches have an ongoing grief or bereavement group. A group for persons who are divorced is another possibility. Parenting groups and groups for persons dealing with substance abuse may be organized.

10. Are the counseling resources in our community adequate? If not,

what can our church do to increase these resources? A task group can be appointed to research this matter, along with the pastor. If resources are inadequate, other churches may be willing to share in developing an ecumenical pastoral counseling center.

Pastoral Calling

In spite of the traditional assumptions and expectations about the value of pastoral calling, it is not as commonly practiced as it once was. There are several reasons for this decline in pastoral calling. Most people, both men and women, are employed outside the home and thus not available during the day to receive a pastoral call. Even many leisure hours are spent away from home. When people are home, a pastoral visit may interrupt household activities. The time demands of the pastoral ministry are great and other responsibilities are given a higher priority than pastoral calling. Like other professionals, many clergy list office hours and expect people to come to the church office to see them. Pastoral calling is apparently not being emphasized in seminary education as it once was. Thus, beginning clergy do not consider pastoral calling important and are not sure how to do it.

Even so, there are some important benefits from pastoral calling that are difficult to attain in any other way:

1. The pastor gets to know the people of the congregation in a way that is not possible through a brief handshake and word of greeting following the worship service.
2. The people get to know their pastor in a much more personal way than simply as that person who leads worship and preaches the sermon.
3. Pastoral calling often reveals needs that would otherwise not be shared with the pastor.
4. The pastoral call is one of the best ways to establish a pastoral relationship so if a crisis arises at a later time, the pastor can minister to the people more effectively.
5. One of the best ways to promote church activities is in the pastoral call. Participation in specific programs can be encouraged and leadership recruited.
6. As a result of a pastoral call, people are likely to support the church more generously. This does not mean that the pastor talks about money, but rather that people develop a more positive atti-

tude toward the church because of the personal interest shown in them by the pastor.

7. Attendance at worship may increase because of pastoral calling. One of the old maxims of pastoral ministry has been that "a home going pastor means a church going congregation."

8. Through visits in homes, the pastor learns of newcomers and others who may be prospective members.

9. From a theological perspective, the minister is a representative of a "seeking God" who goes to the people (see Luke 15). Likewise, the pastor should go to the people and not wait for the people to come.

10. Worship services held in the church building may offer corporate confession, but the home visit provides an opportunity for private confession to occur. This need not be expressed in a formal ritual to be meaningful. Some moments of thoughtful reflection can lead to a few simple sentences spoken aloud. The result can be genuine reconciliation between this person and God or between this person and other persons.

Planning Your Calling

Some pastoral calls cannot be planned. They are made in response to a crisis in the family, such as a serious accident or illness or death. Other contacts are casual or unplanned, for example, when the minister encounters people in unstructured settings yet uses that time to deal with serious concerns of the person.

However, routine calls can be made on a regular basis to some persons or families. For example, there may be a number of people who are either homebound or who live in nursing homes who are visited regularly. A new pastor may develop a plan to visit each person or family in the congregation in order to get acquainted.

Organize your routine calling. Begin with an alphabetical listing of members, and develop a card system or notebook organized by neighborhoods. This saves time and avoids the problem of members who are hurt because you called next door but not at their home. Finding time to call requires self-discipline. You need to set aside certain time slots and hold to them. People appreciate being called ahead of time and asked if the time you have in mind to visit them is convenient. You may want to ask that all members of the family be present unless you are concerned to see one person in particular.

In order to be effective in pastoral calling, pastors need to recognize the difference between a social visit and a pastoral call. One of the differences is certainly the purpose for the visit. In a social call the intention may just be to enjoy being together and discussing topics of mutual interest. Friendship may be a part of the relationship in a pastoral call, but the pastor is also filling a symbolic role. The pastor's symbolic role reminds people of the presence of God in their lives. The pastor also represents the church, the larger community of faith, and can offer the resources of the church to meet the spiritual and other needs of the person or family.

The content of a pastoral call will vary according to the circumstances of each situation. However, the pastor can have in mind a general outline of what should happen. The pastor needs to take the initiative in beginning the conversation. If the visit is the pastor's first, the visit will begin with the pastor establishing rapport and helping everyone get acquainted. The pastor may need to ask questions to encourage people to share pertinent information. The pastor then needs to state the purpose of the visit. The pastor may inquire about a situation within the family that the pastor knows about because it is common knowledge or because it has been discussed before. The pastor can also ask more open-ended questions if there are no specific issues to address. Or there may be some current concern or program of the church that the minister will mention in order to get the conversation going.

Throughout the conversation the pastor should be open to clues about anything that might be troubling this person or family. Previously undisclosed needs of the parishioner may be disclosed to the pastor. Parish calling stands on the boundary of pastoral counseling, and some counseling can take place during the call. Sometimes a pastoral call becomes an intake interview leading to the diagnosis of a problem area and the establishing of a counseling relationship with the pastor or someone else.

The length of the call should be determined by its context. If all seems well with the person or family, twenty minutes may well be sufficient. If problems are present, an hour may be needed. If a serious crisis exists, an even longer time may be required, although an hour should be the normal limit. If problems cannot be resolved in one visit, an appointment can be made to meet again.

The pastor needs to take the initiative in concluding the call. In moving to conclusion, the pastor may wish to summarize what has been discussed or ask the parishioner to state anything that has been agreed upon. Unless the parishioner is a shut-in, the pastor may say, "I hope to see you at the worship service on Sunday." The pastor may wish to leave a resource of some kind, perhaps a daily devotional booklet. The pastor may wish to end the visit with prayer.

Scripture and prayer are important resources for the pastor. Scripture is appropriate in some situations and prayer is appropriate in most. However, Scripture and prayer should neither be automatic nor avoided. Whether to pray and what to pray about should be determined by the context. Many people seem genuinely grateful when their pastor prays with and for them.

Keep a record of your calls and note any special problems. If you need to deal with the problems in some way, do it. Make notes in your datebook or planning calendar about any future appointments you have made and any follow-up you intend to do. Do not trust your memory. It may fail you.

Life-Cycle Needs

Even people who are not members turn to the church at times of special need, and sometimes those needs develop at times of transition. It has been said that people look to the church when it's time to "hatch, match, and dispatch." Pregnancy, birth, marriage, and death, as well as other life-changing events may offer the opportunity or need for pastoral care. Divorce, serious illness, accidents, crime, storm damage, and fire are other events that can cause people grief. Unemployment and poverty can create a crisis, as well. The church provides rituals and ceremonies to deal with the life-cycle experiences, and the church is devising rituals for some of the other life-changing events, as well.

Birth

In the matters of pregnancy and birth, there are major concerns that a pastor may be called upon to address. If the parents-to-be are not to be married, and particularly if they are teenagers, questions about adoption or abortion may be asked. In the more traditional family of husband and wife, the pregnancy and birth of a child are likely to be anticipated with joy. Yet there are financial and work implications involved. A welcome pregnancy might end in a miscarriage or with a stillbirth. The pastor needs to be prepared to help parents deal with whatever circumstances may arise in connection with pregnancy and birth. The advent of more women in the ministry may help initiate and strengthen ministry to the expectant mother, as well as to the father.

A request to the pastor to baptize a child provides a great opportunity to strengthen the pastoral relationship. The pastor can make an appointment to meet with the parents in their home. The pastor can explore with the parents some of their concerns related to the new child as well as interpret the significance of baptism. Such a personal home visit should be in addition to any instruction for baptism that takes place in a class that might be offered in a larger church.

Religious denominations that do not baptize infants usually have a service for the dedication of infants. Such a service provides a similar opportunity to deepen the pastoral relationship with a family. Likewise, when the child is old enough to be eligible for believers' baptism, a wonderful opportunity is provided for spiritual counseling and guidance.

Marriage

Marriage offers another occasion when persons are open to receiving counseling and guidance as they plan their wedding and anticipate sharing their lives as husband and wife. Even though some of the couples who come to be married are already living together, they still need premarital counseling. A review of the marriage ceremony itself can provide an outline for premarital counseling. The couple needs to be helped to understand the significance of the vows they are taking, the promises they are making. Two people can be very much in love but they are still two different individuals, brought up in different homes and often having different habits, attitudes, and values.

Some pastors use an inventory form or questionnaire that the two people fill out separately. The pastor then guides a discussion of those areas where there are sharp differences. Some areas in which attitudes may differ include finances, religion, in-laws, sharing housework, having children, using leisure time, and friendships or activities that do not include the spouse. Other problem areas may emerge as well and need to be discussed so the couple can begin learning how to handle the conflict.

Only a few couples come to the minister asking for guidance about whether they should marry each other. Usually they come having already decided on the date of their wedding and asking if the minister is available to perform the wedding.

If the minister does not know the couple well or at all, they should be asked to tell a little about themselves. The details of the wedding can then be discussed and the minister can assist in the planning. Dealing with the wedding itself puts the couple at ease and then the couple can come to an agreement about premarital counseling. Ministers will find it helpful to have a printed information sheet or folder that states the policy of the church regarding facilities, services, and charges of the minister, organist, and custodian. Some large churches have a wedding coordinator who handles many of the details of the weddings, and the pastor does the counseling and performs the wedding.

Death

Death never happens at a convenient time. Often it seems that funerals come in bunches and when a pastor is already busiest. Yet to the bereaved family, nothing is more important than their grief. The caring pastor will try to respond as soon as possible after being notified of the death. Usually that response is in the form of a personal visit, although in some cases a phone call may precede the visit

In that initial visit the pastor expresses sympathy and finds out if there are ways in which the pastor and the church can be of help. Some discussion of funeral arrangements may take place, and the pastor may read a brief passage of Scripture and almost certainly would offer a prayer. A subsequent visit may be necessary to secure more information about the deceased (if this person is not known by the pastor) and to plan the funeral. In some cases, the pastor will join the surviving spouse or family members at the funeral home to make arrangements.

Much of the pastoral care and counseling will take place after the funeral or memorial service. The formula 1-1-1-1 (one day, one week, one month, one year) is a good reminder to the pastor to provide follow-up ministry with the bereaved. Unless the bereaved person has temporarily left the community to be with family or friends, the minister should make some contact the day after the funeral just to see how the person is doing. Likewise, one week, one month and then one year after the death, the minister should make contact with the widowed spouse or bereaved parent. Printed resources can be shared. Other persons can be encouraged to provide friendship and support for the bereaved. A telephone call from another church member to say "I'll pick you up on Sunday and take you to church" can mean a lot. The pastor may need to help organize this kind of caring.

Contemporary Concerns

In addition to the pastoral counseling related to birth, marriage, and death, pastors are responding to concerns that they were not previously asked to address, such as family abuse and violence, sexual harassment, homosexuality and homophobia, AIDS, issues related to longer life expectancies, and unemployment.

Some of these are not new concerns, but a greater awareness of their existence and importance has emerged. Fortunately, new resources, including articles, books, seminars, and workshops are being provided to equip the pastor to deal with these concerns.

While they are responding to individual needs, pastors are becoming more aware of the impact the broader society has upon individuals. In his book, *Care of Persons, Care of Worlds,* Larry K. Graham reminds us that pastoral care and counseling must be placed in the context of the larger world in which we live. When developing guidelines for pastoral care, says Dr. Graham, one of the important sources of knowledge is "the social and cultural context in which the act of ministry occurs." Among the other sources cited by Graham are "the living religious tradition," and "the personhood of the caretaker and pastoral theologian."[1] Dr. Graham's book helps us recognize the complexity of the pastoral care of persons. The pastoral care giver must not make the mistake of dealing with an individual in isolation from the persons, ideas, values, and systems that have shaped that person's life. Furthermore, the religious community needs to exert its influence on these social systems that impact our lives, seeking to make these systems positive rather than negative. As the title of the book suggests, we are entrusted with the care of worlds as well as of persons.

Relationship of Pastoral Care to Other Ministries

Although the various aspects of parish ministry are being considered separately in this book, they really exist as part of an integrated whole. Pastoral care, for example, is related to other expressions of ministry in a local church.

Worship provides pastoral care when confession is made and words of absolution are spoken. Prayer, music, times of silence, fellowship with other worshipers, and times to share joys and concerns can all be experienced as pastoral care. The sermon can be a form of group counseling, as was so ably demonstrated by Dr. Harry Emerson Fosdick, distinguished pastor and preacher at Riverside Church in New York for many years.[2] A request for further conversation or counseling following a sermon is not unusual. While it may not happen after every sermon, preachers have found that the sermon can motivate people to contact the minister for personal conversation or counseling.

Similar linkages can be made between pastoral care, administration, and evangelism. Administration provides leadership opportunities that can help members develop self-confidence. Prior to the start of a group's business session, time can be taken to recognize individual concerns and joys. Prayer can be offered on behalf of persons in need. Evangelism takes place when people find that their needs are being addressed. Some of those needs are dealt with best in a counseling session. Visitation is really a form of evangelism, as new relationships are formed and prior relationships strengthened.

Education is absolutely essential in a comprehensive program of pastoral care. Classes and support groups dealing with a variety of topics and needs can be organized. One pastor developed what he called a counseling bookshelf.[3] When he counseled people they sometimes asked if he charged a fee. He said no but suggested that they might want to contribute toward the cost of maintaining the counseling bookshelf. Books appropriate to the specific need were loaned, or in some cases, given to the person. Thus, pastoral care can be extended beyond the limitations of the pastor's own time and strength.

8

Worship

Søren Kierkegaard contrasted the drama of worship with the drama that takes place on the stage of a theater. The secular drama includes the person "who sits and prompts by whispers," the actor "who strides out prominently," and the theatergoers "who are to pass judgment on the artist." Of course, "no one is so foolish as to regard the prompter as more important than the actor."[1]

In regard to worship, says Kierkegaard, many people make the mistake of looking on the speaker as an actor and themselves as theatergoers who are there to pass judgment on the speaker. But in worship the speaker is not the actor. Rather, the speaker is the prompter, giving the people their lines to speak. The stage is eternity, and the listener stands before God during the talk. The role of the prompter is to help the listener become the true actor. Perhaps the phenomenon of equating worship and entertainment is an even greater problem now than it was in Kierkegaard's day, for many people still fail to distinguish clearly between entertainment and worship. Leaders of worship as well as listeners may be at fault here. Worship can become a spectator sport, with listeners thinking their role is to pass judgment on the quality of the performance they observed.

What Is Worship?

Perhaps the simplest definition of worship is that given by Evelyn Underhill in her classic book entitled simply *Worship*: "Worship in all its grades and kinds, is the response of the creature to the eternal."[2] God initiates the relationship and we human beings respond to this seeking God. The revelation of God in Jesus Christ shapes our Christian understanding of worship.

"Celebration" has become popular in recent years as a way to describe worship. Our worship should be joyous because we have much to celebrate. However, there is a danger that we will emphasize *how* we celebrate and not *what* we celebrate. The possibility also exists that we may end up celebrating our culture or even ourselves instead of God. The title of the book *Celebration of the Gospel* reminds us what it is we celebrate. We celebrate the Gospel, the good news of God's victory over sin and death in Christ Jesus.[3]

We often refer to the worship event as a worship service. The word *service* suggests doing something for others, "whether we speak of a secretarial service, the Forest service, or a catering service."[4] Closely linked to the word *service* is the word *liturgy.* Liturgy is sometimes defined as a particular form of public worship. S. T. Ritenour offers a simple yet comprehensive definition, saying that "liturgy is what people do and say in corporate worship."[5] James F. White reminds us that the origin of our modern word *liturgy* "is the Greek word *leitourgia,* from the words for work (*ergon*) and people (*laos*)."[6] Thus the liturgy is intended to be the work of the people. We should think of a liturgical service as one in which those present are fully involved in the experience. Worshipers should be participants rather than spectators.

The Content of Worship

The experience of the young man Isaiah in the temple, as recorded in Isaiah 6:1-8, has become a kind of motif or outline for Christian worship. Isaiah's experience suggests that in worship we symbolically look in three directions: upward, inward, and outward.

In Isaiah's vision he first sees "the Lord sitting upon a throne high and lifted up." The angels sing, "Holy, holy, holy is the Lord of hosts." As we enter into the experience of worship we should sense that we are in the presence of God. In a symbolic upward look, we acknowledge with reverence (love and awe) that we have come to worship God. Our response is one of *adoration and praise.*

The upward look is followed by the inward look. When Isaiah in his vision sees the Lord of hosts, Isaiah suddenly becomes aware of his sinfulness. "Woe is me," he says, "For I am lost, for I am a man of unclean lips and I dwell in the midst of a people of unclean lips." Isaiah does not first point to the sins of others, but rather, he acknowledges his own shortcomings, because, he says, "my eyes have seen the king, the lord of hosts."

Confession is not a popular thing to do. In what other setting do people come together weekly to say, "God, I'm not as good as I ought to be. Help me to be a little better"? We can come to a worship service feeling comfortable and complacent about ourselves, yet in the light of God's love and purity we realize our unworthiness and are moved to confession. Such confrontation and confession may be the reason some people stay away from corporate worship. They do not want to admit that what they say and do and think is displeasing to God.

Yet there is good news. Isaiah's confession is followed by a symbolic act of cleansing and forgiveness. Isaiah is told, "Your guilt is taken away, and your sin forgiven." In our worship there must be a time for *confession and forgiveness*. If we give people the opportunity to confess their sins, we must also offer them the words of assurance and pardon.

The final look in worship is the outward look. Only after Isaiah has "seen the Lord high and lifted up"; only after Isaiah has looked deep into his own soul, examining his conscience, making confession and receiving forgiveness; only then is Isaiah ready to hear the voice of the Lord, saying, "Whom shall I send, and who will go for us?" Isaiah responds, "Here am I. Send me." True worship includes *proclamation and response,* commitment and dedication, the willingness to be of service to persons in need. Worship must not become escapism. The journey inward must be followed by the journey outward.

Although the experience of Isaiah is that of an individual rather than a community and is recorded in the Hebrew Bible rather than the New Testament, the basic outline of true worship is present. Another insight into Christian worship is found in the experience of the two travelers on the road to Emmaus following the resurrection of Jesus (Luke 24:13-35). As they walk along, Jesus joins them, but they do not recognize him. Not until they sit together at the table, when Jesus takes the bread, blesses it, breaks it, and gives it to them, do they recognize him (Luke 24:31). In Christian worship we can experience the presence of Christ; in the sharing of the Eucharist (the Holy Communion), Christ can become real to us. Once we have experienced Christ in our lives, we want to share the good news with others. As someone has put it, "We enter to worship. We depart to serve."

Making Worship Meaningful

Sometimes people describe their worship experience primarily in terms of likes and dislikes: "I liked the choir anthem. I didn't like the sermon" (or vice versa). Seldom do they take time to be more analytical in their response to a worship experience. If worship is to meet the needs of the people, a process of evaluation must be utilized. Small group discussions, open forums, and questionnaires are ways this evaluation can take place. For evaluations to have depth and to be helpful, here are six criteria that may be helpful in planning and evaluating our corporate worship.[7]

1. Our worship should be *informed by the past.* Sometimes we start planning our worship as though there are no historical precedents. We can learn from the past and be guided by what other generations have found meaningful. Some components of worship have withstood the test of time. We need not be bound by tradition but we can be enlightened by it. Indeed, some of the current reforms in worship are in reality a return to earlier forms.

2. Our worship should be *theologically sound.* In our worship we are acknowledging the worth of the God we worship. As we plan and evaluate our worship, we need to reflect upon our understanding of God. What is the nature of this supreme being? In what way are we as human beings related to God, the object of our worship? How can we best express this relationship? What are we saying about God and about ourselves in the content and actions of our worship? Is our worship distinctively Christian?

3. Our worship must be *relevant to life.* What current events are shaping our lives and our world? How does what we talk about and experience on Sunday relate to what we say and do during the other days of the week? Jesus used the stuff of everyday life in his parables—a lost coin, a lost sheep, a lost son, soils and seeds, fig trees and vines. Our worship needs to help us see the relationship between the sacred and the secular, between God and daily life.

4. Our worship must be *meaningful to those present.* This goal may never be fully achieved, but we surely must strive to attain it. When you plan your worship service, imagine who will be present. These are people with fears, needs, hopes. They may be experiencing joy or sorrow in their lives. They represent different ages, education, occupations. What words, what illustrations or references will be most meaningful to this particular congregation?

5. *Involve the congregation.* Are the laity genuinely participating in the worship service? Are people fully involved? If not, how could they be? A children's class can compose a prayer and lead the congregation in praying in unison. A family can bring forward a loaf of homemade bread and the cup for Communion. Or a family can light the candles on the Advent wreath. Be imaginative and the possibilities are endless!

6. Our worship should *result in a sense of mission.* The real test of whether our worship is valid is what we do when we leave the place of worship. Has our worship changed us in any way? Have we confronted God and our own sinfulness? Have we received God's cleansing and grace? Are we ready to do God's will, take on the difficult task, respond to the desperate needs of the world?

We need to be challenged, as well as comforted, in our worship. Worship must never become an escape from the problems of the world. Rather, as in the case of Isaiah, our encounter with God and our self-examination should lead to an awareness of a world in need. We then should be able to see how we can respond to that need in some meaningful way.

Planning the Order of Worship

Worship is the central activity of the church and usually involves more people than any other program of the church. Whether you use a book of worship that provides the form for your major worship services or you develop your own, serious planning is vital if a worship service is to happen as it should. Usually the pastor is the person who must initiate this planning process and carry decisions through to completion.

Even pastors whose denominations prescribe the form of the worship service will find helpful the ten steps suggested by The Section on Worship of the General Board of Discipleship of the United Methodist Church.[8]

1. *Plan ahead.* The church year with its various seasons, such as Advent, Epiphany, and Lent, provides a basis for planning. Plan for a whole season at a time. At least eight weeks before the season begins, set aside at least a half day to do preliminary planning. Be sure to note any special services in that season in addition to Sunday. Make a work sheet for every service, and begin a file folder for each service in which you collect all the resources you discover.

2. *Choose scripture lessons.* If you use the common lectionary, list the passages (Old Testament, Psalm, Epistle, and Gospel) on your work sheet. Read the passages and determine which one will be the foundation for the service. Mark that passage with an asterisk.

3. *Choose the sermon focus.* Determine the basic image, thrust, statement, or impact that will guide the sermon preparation and give direction to the service. Ask, How does the scripture passage affect me and this congregation? Where does the passage challenge? Where does it comfort? What responses does the scripture passage call forth? State the sermon focus in a short, declarative sentence. Sermon ideas should be collected and placed in the file folder.

4. *Consider any special emphasis.* Will the service have some special emphasis? Is there Holy Communion, a baptism, installation of officers, dedication of a memorial gift? Will a special group be present, requiring some type of recognition?

5. *Schedule a planning meeting.* Schedule a meeting with the musician(s) and the worship planning team, if there is one, at least eight weeks before the season begins. Unfortunately, some clergy plan worship without consultation, much to the frustration of musicians and others who have leadership responsibility. Remember, liturgy is the work of the people. If your church has a the worship committee, involve them in this planning process (see below).

6. *Prepare for and hold the planning meeting.* Duplicate the worksheets for each service and distribute them to the planning team. Then everyone at the meeting can work together to complete the planning.

7. *Select hymns.* The hymns should reflect and enhance the scripture lessons, the sermon focus, or the service emphasis. Often the first hymn is a hymn of praise; the second related to the sermon; and the third a response to the Word, a Communion hymn, or a hymn of sending forth.

8. *Choose anthem(s), service/Communion music, and instrumental music.* Musicians and pastor(s) should work together to create an environment of sound that enhances this particular worship service. This is an opportunity to be creative. For example, brass instruments could be used on Easter morning to help announce

the joy of the resurrection. Choose any special singers or instrumentalists, and contact them well in advance.

9. *Select other worship leaders.* Lay liturgists, readers, acolytes, Communion servers, ushers, and greeters should be designated and trained. Other participants such as sacred dancers and other artists should be chosen as well, if they are to share in the service. Include persons of all ages and conditions. A group of children in a church school class can lead the congregation in a litany of thanksgiving they have written. An individual can share a creed or a personal testimony she or he has written. Contact these persons in advance and give them a copy of the worksheet for the service in which they will have part.

10. *Determine visuals.* Keeping in mind the liturgical color for the season, work with the flower coordinator, altar guild, or florist to select appropriate flowers or table settings. The church may have banners appropriate to the season, or some could be made. A rugged cross can be constructed or a paschal candle used. A harvest display at Thanksgiving time will be appreciated.

While these ten steps can be modified to fit a particular pastor and congregation, they suggest how the worship life of the congregation can be strengthened with planning. Too often the pastor does all the worship planning alone, and it becomes a burden instead of a joy. Making the planning a team experience may not lessen the time involved for the pastor, but it can surely enrich the worship of the people.

In addition to these ten steps, several more need to be taken as the time of the worship service draws nearer. The pastor needs to prepare the prayers as well as the sermon. A final check with participants is helpful, and some services may require a rehearsal. Just prior to the service, all leaders should meet to review their responsibilities. The pastor or someone else should offer a prayer asking for God's blessing and guidance as these persons lead others in worship.

The Worship Committee

Some denominations provide for a worship committee in their local church organizational structure, others do not. Even if such a committee is not a denominational requirement, a congregation may wish to form such a group.

Some ministers seem to be threatened by having an active worship committee or task group. The pastor may feel her or his authority to plan and conduct worship will be challenged or usurped by the small group. Such feelings are understandable, but the pastor who does not utilize the laity in this important area of worship makes a serious mistake. Even the pastor of a very small church (which perhaps cannot justify a separate worship committee) can see that the worship work area is included in the responsibilities of some group in the church.

Some ways a lay committee can be of help to the pastor in regard to worship are

1. *Planning.* Lay members of the committee can offer ideas and suggest resources during the planning of worship events. Committee members may be aware of possible schedule conflicts.

2. *Consulting.* The lay committee can be a sounding board for new ideas or programs, such as the use of sacred dance in a worship service. The pastor would be wise to discuss ideas with the committee and thus create understanding and support for proposals.

3. *Experimenting.* One worship committee opened each of its meetings with a worship experience led by a member of the committee. The committee members were encouraged to introduce something new and different into this worship experience. The idea was to try out some things to see if they could be included in services of the congregation.

4. *Recruiting.* People are needed to do a lot of things related to worship, such as being greeters, ushers, communion stewards and/or servers, musicians, and lay readers. The committee members themselves can do some of these things and can also recruit other people to assume these responsibilities.

5. *Communicating.* If they have helped do the planning, the members of the committee will feel a sense of ownership of the worship plans of the congregation. They can communicate plans informally to others. They can help with publicity, including posters, announcements, newspaper releases, newsletter items, photographs, and letters.

6. *Evaluating.* This committee can serve as a liaison between pastor and congregation. People may be unhappy with some aspect of the worship service but be reluctant to voice their complaint to the pastor. However, the unhappy person may be willing to speak to a worship committee member if anonymity is maintained. The pastor should be able to get good, honest feedback from the lay com-

mittee about the worship program of the church and the pastor's role as worship leader. If further data is desired, the committee and the pastor can design a questionnaire or arrange an open forum.

Some churches have a group in the church known as the altar guild, which usually has a more narrowly defined list of tasks than the worship committee. These tasks may include securing and arranging flowers or other special artistic displays, preparing the elements for Communion (and cleaning communionware afterward), making sure the candles are ready to be lit, and hanging paraments of the correct color for the liturgical season in the chancel.

Larger churches may have other committees or organized groups such as a music committee, ushers group, greeters group, and flower committee. These groups can be represented on the worship committee, and the worship committee can oversee their activities.

Making Changes in Worship

The seven last words of the church, according to someone are, We have never done it that way. Human beings are creatures of habit and find comfort in the familiar. Change tends to be resisted in the church more than in some other institutions, perhaps because the church is seen as a conserver of values, and change can be seen as a letting go of important values.

A church I once served wanted to remodel the chancel area that was cluttered with flags, banners, chancel furniture, and chairs for the choir. The congregation engaged for a very modest sum an architect who visited the church and made recommendations. One of the recommendations was that the hymn boards on either side of the chancel be removed. There was an outcry of indignation from several people. The architect asked, "Do you have a printed bulletin that gives the hymn numbers?" "Yes, almost always," they replied. "Are the hymns announced aloud?" "Yes," they answered. "Then why do you need the two hymn boards?" asked the architect. "Because we have always had them" they somewhat weakly replied.

In the process of remodeling the chancel, the hymn boards somehow got lost and never did get put back. One of the trustees accepted the blame for this act of "carelessness," and to my knowledge, no one stopped attending worship because of this change, although a few people were unhappy for a while.

We tend to absolutize the forms of worship. We make absolute (sacred) the way we conduct our worship. We forget that the forms we use are only the means to an end—that end being the worship of God. We even make sacred the way the space is arranged for worship. Thus, changing the arrangement of the chancel is like rearranging the furniture in heaven.

One of the recent changes in worship is the shift to inclusive language, both in references to humankind and to God. People are having more difficulty accepting inclusive language for human beings than for references to God. That is understandable because language is more than words. A whole set of meanings and values is attached to our use of words. Therefore, the language used in worship raises profound theological concerns and not only ethical or moral questions of fairness. The matter of using inclusive language deserves more discussion than this one chapter allows. However, let us suppose that a pastor wishes to lead a congregation toward greater acceptance of inclusive language in worship. Here are some general principles about change that the pastor should keep in mind.

1. *Start where the people are, not where you are.* Begin by finding out the attitudes of the members of the congregation. It is arrogant for the pastor to assume that only he or she knows what is right and best for this congregation. The pastor's ideas have been shaped over a period of years by influences that members of the congregation have not experienced.

2. *Exercise patience.* This is a corollary of the first principle. Do not expect people to change instantly simply because you tell them they should. Most of those people were in the church before you came and will be there after you leave.

3. *Be cautious about cashing your "authority check."* The pastor does have some authority that can be used to make decisions. Like the checks in a checkbook, once a check is cashed, the money is no longer available. Likewise, the pastor must choose carefully how and when to use pastoral authority. For the pastor to insist on his or her viewpoint when the majority of the congregation disagrees with that position may not be a wise use of authority.

4. *Take the congregation with you.* Work with the worship committee or a special task group where some serious discussion can take place. Together the pastor and people can design a program of study. A number of resources for study are available.[9]

5. *Be creative in instituting language changes without flaunting change.* Changing the Lord's Prayer or the baptismal formula may bring an instant negative reaction. However, in other aspects of worship inclusive language can be used in a way that does not call attention to itself. For example, in addressing God in prayer, many of God's attributes that are not gender exclusive may be used. For example, God may be referred to as "Creator of the universe."

6. *Be a good pastor.* Do as well as you can all the things that a pastor is expected to do. By providing good pastoral care, you will gain the trust and respect of your people. Even though they may not agree with you, they are much more likely to listen to you without becoming angry when you speak of the need for change.

When proposing changes both pastor and people need to remember the words of St. Paul, "Love does not insist on its own way" (1 Cor. 13:5).

Leading Worship

After all the necessary planning of a worship service has taken place, there finally comes that moment when the worship leader must walk into the chancel and lead the service. How well the leader conducts the service is important in determining whether this gathering of people becomes a worshiping community. To lead others effectively in worship, the leader must be

1. Prepared. Although the preparation for worship must begin long before the time of worship, the leader should arrive early to make sure everything is in order for the worship service. Practice the whole service in the empty church, either by yourself or with other persons who have special leadership roles. Even if you do not practice the service in the church, go through the service carefully in your mind so you know exactly what you are doing. Grady Hardin in his book, *The Leadership of Worship* says: "Worship leaders should anticipate the services they plan to lead until they have already worshiped in them in their imagination. The parts of the service should be so well rehearsed that the leader can participate fully and at the same time be alert to small details."[10]

2. Poised. You are much more likely to be poised if you have done a good job of preparing. Preparation gives you a sense of confidence in what you are doing. This self-confidence (not arrogance or self-right-eousness) is reassuring to the congregation.

If at all possible, allow yourself some time just before the service begins when you can prepare yourself emotionally and spiritually. Take your time as you lead worship. Do not rush, even if you feel pressured by the clock. Stay calm if the unexpected happens. You should have an idea of what you would do if an there is an emergency, such as a power failure, an interruption in the service, a sudden illness, or a fire.

As you lead the service, give clear instructions. Practice what you will say in the various parts of the service, such as welcoming visitors, announcing the offering, introducing the scripture lessons, or giving directions about how Communion will be served.

3. Pleasant. Offer hospitality and friendliness. The pastor need not be casual, flippant, or irreverent. Worship is a serious activity, but we can be joyful and pleasant. We should affirm the words of Scripture, "I was glad when they said unto me, let us go into the house of the Lord."

Be natural in voice and manner. Avoid what is sometimes called "the stained glass voice." Perhaps because of a sense of awe about being the one speaking for God to all these people, a worship leader may take on a very unnatural tone of voice. This is not helpful because it calls atten-tion to the person speaking rather than to the content of the message. There is such a thing as getting in the way of worship rather than aiding it. Do not try to make clever or humorous remarks. Remember, you are the prompter, not the actor. Worship is not entertainment. The wor-shipers are the actors.

The drama we call worship should be one of the most exciting and important events that we experience as Christians. In worship we come together as a community of faith, the body of Christ. The pastor of a congregation is privileged to be the prompter who gives the members of the congregation their lines, so they can act out their Christian faith on the stage called life.

9

Preaching

The number one requirement of pastors cited by many church leaders is *good preaching*[1] Yet not too many years ago preaching was under attack as an outmoded and ineffective means of communication. This negative attitude toward preaching emerged in the late '60s and early '70s when many traditional values, customs, and institutions were called into question. In addition to the cultural changes taking place in our society in the '60s and '70s a communications revolution was taking place. The advent of television into our homes had begun to change the way we perceived reality. Events happening across the ocean in another continent were flashed on the screen in our living room. The concept of the global village emerged, and our world consciousness was heightened. There was a sense of immediacy about events that newsprint and radio had not provided.

Not only has television changed the way we perceive reality, but it has reduced the time needed to convey a message. Television commercials are often as short as fifteen seconds, whereas sermons are measured in minutes. (Of course, it has been said that what matters is not how long the sermon is, but how long it seems.) Television even provides stay-at-home worship services for those persons unable to come to church.

Preachers have responded to the crisis in communications in a variety of ways. Some of these responses have been well received and some have not. In one suburban congregation, the pastor invited the congregation to vote on two options when the time came for the sermon—the pastor would preach a sermon, or the pastor would briefly introduce some ideas from the sermon and then receive questions and comments from the worshipers. The minister seemed disappointed when the congregation voted overwhelmingly for the traditional sermon.

In the late '70s and early '80s the attitude toward the sermon changed in a positive way. As Ernest Campbell puts it in a lecture at Garrett-Evangelical Theological Seminary, "The picture has *brightened.* The fall has been followed by a rise." Dr. Campbell makes a further observation, stating that "when preaching began to suffer some demise, it was an inside job. Lay people have always put the ability to preach right near the top of what they wish in a pastor."[2]

Creativity and Preaching

The communications revolution challenges the preacher to be creative in order to attract and hold the attention of the congregation. While in one sense creativity is a gift, we can do much to stimulate the gift that is already within us as creatures of God. We can be helped in this effort by appropriating research findings about how our brain works. Sidney Parnes, Ruth Noller, and Angelo Biondi, in their book *Guide to Creative Action,* tell us:

> The essence of the concept of creativity might be considered to be the association of thoughts, ideas, etc. into a new and relevant configuration—one that has meaning beyond the sum of the parts—that provides a synergistic effect.[3]

This association of thoughts can be better understood by turning to the recent studies of the differing functions of the two halves of our brains.

To summarize briefly, "Researchers discovered that each side of the brain has its own areas of specialization and processes information in its own way." In a normally functioning brain, there is a mass of nerve fibers called the corpus Callosum, which bridges the two hemispheres of the brain. Thus, the two sides of the brain work together for almost every activity, although one hemisphere or the other usually predominates for a particular task. Marilee Zdenek points out:

> In 95% of the population, it is the left hemisphere that remembers names, adds columns of numbers, computes time and works in a logical, linear fashion. The right hemisphere is the mysterious, artistic side of the brain where metaphors are understood and emotions are realized. It's where dreams and imagery occur and fantasies are born."[4]

Zdenek reports on her interviews with a number of famous creative persons, including Charles Schulz, the cartoonist who created Charlie Brown, Lucy, Snoopy, and the other characters of "Peanuts." When she asked him where he gets the ideas for his comic strip, he replied, "When

I'm partaking in any sport or activity I'll almost always get some kind of idea. Attending a symphony, playing tennis. I'm always coining little phrases." On the basis of such comments, Zdenek advises, "Relax the left hemisphere enough and the unconscious ideas begin to surface."[5]

Her comment is significant for preaching. In order to be creative, we need to de-emphasize the left brain functions and allow the intuitive ideas and thoughts to surface to our consciousness. We need to dream and fantasize a bit—use our imagination. Ideas for sermons can come from a great variety of places and experiences.

For the preacher, the creative process involves an encounter with the Word as the preacher tries to discover the truths that are relevant to the needs of the people to whom she or he will preach. When the preacher becomes totally absorbed, caught up, in this encounter with truth, there is "an intensity of awareness, and heightened consciousness."[6] To use God language, we might say the Holy Spirit is at work, intensifying this encounter with biblical truth. (Zdenek in her book speaks of the Muse within each of us, but for the Christian preacher to speak of the indwelling presence of the Holy Spirit seems more appropriate.) When this deep absorption occurs, real creativity can take place.

Rollo May notes that an artist (or you and I), in moments of intense encounter, experiences neurological changes such as quickened heart beat; higher blood pressure, increased intensity, and constriction of vision. We may become oblivious to things around us, even the passage of time. While these may seem like the symptoms of anxiety, May says what the creative person is feeling is joy ("defined as the emotion that goes with heightened consciousness, the mood that accompanies the experience of actualizing one's own potentialities").[7]

Some barriers to creative preaching need to be acknowledged and overcome. One barrier is that both the congregation and the preacher are likely to be uncomfortable with innovative approaches or methods. To overcome this barrier, congregation and preacher need to open themselves to the possibility of new ways of communicating the gospel.

A second barrier is that the preacher may not think of himself or herself as a truly creative person. Through the educational process we are so strongly indoctrinated with the ideas of others that our own creativity is stifled. We may not sufficiently trust our own intuition and feelings. The preacher needs to study the theories of creativity, such as the implications of left brain-right brain research, and begin to exercise his or her own creative ability.

A third barrier to creativity in preaching is lack of prepara[tion]. Ministers constantly complain about lack of time for reading [and ser]mon preparation. The demands on a pastor are enormous, but [the min]ister must recognize the possibility that the problem may be poor time management and that priorities need to be reconsidered. Overcoming this barrier also may require educating the congregation about how sermons are created. Lay people place great importance on preaching but often have no clear idea of the amount of time involved in preparing the sermon to preach.

The minister who wishes to be a creative preacher must have a place and a time where this creative process can have a chance to happen. He or she also needs to receive the stimulation of new ideas and thoughts. Such ideas can come from a variety of experiences, including reading that may not be specifically classified as religious. A period of incubation can help bring about creativity. If an idea is present in the mind, over a period of time the principle of serendipity can come into play. (The word "serendipity" is attributed to the princes of Serendip, who had the ability to make unexpected discoveries of things they were not looking for while they were looking for something else.) That is, the preacher who has a sermon idea in mind will come across other ideas and experiences related to the sermon topic. This only happens if there is a sufficient amount of time between the initial idea and the actual writing and delivery of the sermon.

The Christian Tradition of Preaching

Not only are today's preachers called to be creative, but they also follow in a long tradition that goes back to the Hebrew prophets who brought God's message to the people, calling the people to righteous living, and warning the people of dire consequences if they did not respond.

John the Baptist is seen as a transitional person between the Hebrew prophets and Jesus and the disciples. Mark's gospel says that "after John was arrested, Jesus came into Galilee, preaching the gospel of God"(Mark 1:14). Jesus preached wherever people gathered, including the synagogue and outdoors. Peter's Pentecost sermon is an example of early Christian preaching, presenting the gospel message calling for acceptance of the truth of salvation through Christ and repentance. Peter's sermon is designed to bring about conversion. C. H. Dodd in his landmark book, *The Apostolic Preaching and its Developments,* identifies this kind of preaching as *kerygma*. He contrasts it with *didache,* the teaching of the church. According to Dodd, "Much of our preaching in church at the present day would not have been recognized by the early Christians as kerygma. It is teaching, or exhortation, or what is called *homilia,* that is, the more or less informal discussion of various aspects of Christian life and thought, addressed to a congregation already established in the faith."[8] Even though much of our present-day preaching may indeed be didache, we need to remember to share the *kerygma,* the gospel of our Lord.

Types of Sermons

The link between the Bible and preaching has been strongly forged through centuries of use. Martin Luther, the great reformer, emphasized the importance of preaching, along with the sacraments. For many preachers, preaching must be biblical preaching, or it is not really preaching. Although sermons may be biblically based, they can vary in regard to content, structure, and delivery. The preferences of the preacher and the expectations of the congregation will influence the form the sermon takes. Among the types of sermons preached today, one can find sermons that can be labeled exegetical, expository, textual, doctrinal, situational, topical, narrative, and dialogue. These sermon classifications are not clear cut, and other persons may use other terms or describe them differently. However, following are my descriptions of each of these types of sermons.

The *exegetical* sermon usually takes a passage of Scripture and moves through it verse by verse, explaining and expounding on the truth contained in the verses. A passage from the epistles lends itself well to exegetical preaching. A strength of this method is that people can follow the sermon in their own Bibles. Another strength is that people get to know a specific passage of Scripture quite well. A weakness of the method may be that it lacks the structure or cohesiveness usually expected in a sermon. The verse-by-verse approach may seem to require less preparation, and thus the resulting commentary could lack depth and focus.

Obviously, every sermon that uses biblical material requires exegetical work by the preacher. The question then becomes, How much of the exegetical material is included in the sermon? Does the verse-by-verse exegesis of a passage of Scripture really constitute a sermon? Most preachers would say no. More has to be done to create a sermon that will hold the attention of the hearers and make a connection with their daily lives. Thus, this method is probably used more often in a Bible study than in a sermon.

In the *expository* sermon the preacher deals with the passage of Scripture as a whole, exposing the truth the passage contains. A parable of Jesus, an act of healing, an encounter, or a conversation may provide the basis for an expository sermon. This kind of sermon requires more preparation because the preacher has to decide what central truth should be shared. Likewise, the preacher needs to be clear about the desired response from the listeners. What does the preacher want them to know, be, or do?

A *textual* sermon takes a shorter passage of Scripture, usually only a verse or two, discovering the truth expressed in that verse and expounding on it. For example, the golden rule (Luke 6:31) or one of the Beatitudes (Matt. 5:3-11) could become the inspiration for an entire sermon. This is a traditional approach to preaching. Some verses of Scripture lend themselves to a clear outline that forms the framework of the sermon. The textual sermon allows the preacher considerable freedom to expand on the central thought in the text. A danger with the textual sermon is that the preacher may read much more into the text than is really there. Another danger is that the text is mentioned and then seemingly forgotten as the sermon unfolds.

While the *doctrinal* sermon may draw heavily on Scripture, the primary concern of the sermon is to explain and make relevant a particular belief or doctrine of the church. Such doctrines as sin, grace, or salvation need to be explained to people. However, it is important to realize that a doctrine is an "intellectual formulation of an experience," and thus the preacher needs to deal not only with the intellectual formulation but also with the experience that led to the doctrinal statement.

The *life situation* sermon is associated with Harry Emerson Fosdick, who contended that too many sermons start in Galilee and stay in Galilee, and do not make a connection between the biblical material and the problems that people face in their daily lives. Fosdick suggested that preachers start with the real problems of our society and of individual persons.[9]

The task of the preacher then is to shed light on dealing with the problem, using the Bible and whatever other sources are available.

Fosdick was severely criticized by some persons for his ideas, but others felt he was on the right track. His own preaching reflected his concern to make the gospel relevant to the life situations of the people in the pew. Life situation sermons can deal with such personal problems as anger, loneliness, and fear, or with such societal problems as medical ethics, crime, capital punishment, or violence in television programs.

In a *topical* sermon the preacher focuses on a topic or theme, rather than a specific verse or passage of Scripture. Sometimes sermons begin with a text but the text is only a launching pad for an idea the preacher wants to develop. If the text were omitted and the sermon still seemed fairly complete, the sermon would be called topical, rather than textual. While topical sermons allow the preacher to comment on current events or societal and personal issues, some persons believe that the lack of a biblical basis makes this a lecture rather than a sermon. Yet there are times when a topical sermon is acceptable, although I would seek to utilize Scripture in an appropriate way, if at all possible.

The *narrative* or story telling form is one that has a strong biblical precedent. As Bruce Salmon points out in his book, *Storytelling in Preaching,* "Story is the most easily transmitted literary form . . . [It carries] an evocative force beyond that of simple declarative statements." Stories are evocative because they "draw us into the tales. We identify with the characters, we feel the suspense, we get caught up in the action, we resonate with the plot." Thus "the Biblical story becomes our story" and "in the process Scripture becomes forever contemporary."[10] The modern-day preacher can retell a biblical story, perhaps taking the role of one of the characters in the story and speaking in the first-person. However, narrative sermons need not be confined to retelling the biblical story. Other stories can be told as well. Even one's personal story can become a powerful witness.[11]

The *dialogue* sermon is not as common as a sermon preached by one person, but it can be an effective way to communicate. A biblical passage or text can be discussed by two people, each of whom brings a different perspective to the passage. Sometimes controversial subjects can be dealt with more fairly by two persons.

Sermon Preparation

Sermon preparation requires time, lots of time. The rule regarding sermon preparation that was taught to me in seminary was that we need one hour of preparation for each minute of preaching. Thus, a twenty-minute sermon requires an average preparation time of twenty hours. Often that amount of time seems unavailable to the busy pastor. The organization of a sermon, the choice of words, and the sentence structure are vital. Pruning and rewriting are necessary, and those tasks take time as well. The question then becomes, Is preaching really so important that I need to give a significant amount of time to preparation? Scripture and tradition say yes.

Through the sermon, the pastor almost certainly speaks to more people than in any other aspect of ministry. This fact alone makes it imperative that the sermon be carefully prepared and effectively delivered. If people are willing to give their time to listen to the sermon, the preacher must be willing to prepare a sermon that is worthy of the time the people give.

You need a process to organize your time and your thoughts for sermon preparation. The time schedule that works best will vary from person to person. The lectionary is a great help in suggesting scripture passages suitable for each Sunday of the year. If your denomination does not advocate using the common lectionary, you can still work ahead by establishing themes or passages of Scripture that will be the basis of individual sermons or sermon series.

Some pastors find it helpful to take several days for a personal planning retreat to plan their sermon topics for at least a quarter at a time. I know one pastor who planned an entire year of preaching. He then prepared a booklet listing the sermon topic for each Sunday of the year along with additional information, including scripture references and a summary of the content of the sermon. There was space on each page where people of the congregation who received the booklet could jot down questions, comments or illustrations relating to that particular sermon. These booklets were returned to the pastor to assist him in sermon preparation.

Another pastor has what he calls "a sermon garden." He uses manila folders to collect and save ideas for future sermons. The folder for a sermon may at first contain only a title, a quotation, a scriptural text, a cartoon, or a song that captured his attention. He puts this "seed" in the folder and then cultivates his sermon garden by adding other material and ideas that comes to his attention. At any given moment his garden includes seeds just planted, sermons growing well, and some sermons ready to harvest.

When we plan ahead, the principle of serendipity comes into play. Ideas, experiences, quotations, cartoons, news items, and scripture references that would otherwise go unnoticed suddenly become important because they relate to a future sermon. They are saved, placed in the appropriate folder for future use. Connections are made that would not occur if the preacher had not planned ahead.

The process by which a sermon is prepared will vary from person to person. However, let me suggest a process that seems to work well for some pastors.[12]

1.   *Select a Biblical passage or text* you think has a message that you and your hearers need. If you are using the common lectionary, then you will choose from among the suggested passages. Most pastors find it easier to make one of the passages the primary basis of the sermon, rather than trying to combine all three (or four, if the psalm is included) in one sermon.

2.   *Read the passage and its context several times, writing down all the thoughts that occur to you.* It is important that you allow the Scripture to speak to you before you consult the commentaries. Otherwise you may stifle your own creativity by unconsciously deciding the thoughts of others are more important than your own.

3.   *If you can work with the original languages, look up all the key words.* A Bible dictionary may be useful as well. Exegete (discover the critical explanation of) as many of the important phrases and sentences as time permits, making full notes.

4.   *Read books and commentaries on the passage, writing down ideas that seem especially meaningful.* By turning to the books and commentaries, you will gain some new insights about the passage. Also, review your own ideas, jotted down in step 2, to see if you want to change them because of what you have read.

5.   *Think deeply about this scripture passage.* Ask yourself, What is God trying to say to us through this record? What is the word of warning, promise, comfort, hope, or instruction that comes to me from this story? Have I ever had, or do I know of anyone who ever had, a similar experience? Again, jot down thoughts that come to you.

6.   *Having compiled this mass of material, lift out those ideas you want to communicate to your hearers.* Perhaps one central thought will emerge, which then becomes the thesis or proposition of your

sermon. Discard those ideas that do not relate to the message you wish to preach. (You may want to save some of these ideas for future sermons.)

7. *Arrange in some meaningful order the ideas you wish to use.* Try to express these ideas in a series of clear statements, each of which can be developed. These become the main points of your sermon.

8. *Work on the conclusion of your sermon.* Conclusions often are the weakest part of the sermon. The preacher runs out of time and so ends the sermon too abruptly, or the conclusion is not really a conclusion but rather a final new point to be made. The preacher needs to decide early in the process what response is called for by this message and the best way to state this.

9. *Work on the introduction of the sermon.* Ask, How can I arouse the interest of my hearers in these ideas? How can I convince people right at the start that this sermon is important and they should listen attentively?

10. *Write out the sermon in full.* Not everybody agrees with this step because it is time consuming, and the preacher may then be tempted to read the sermon word for word. However, failure to write the sermon in full may lead to awkward sentence structure, weak content, lack of proportion in the various parts of the sermon, and a rambling style of delivery. Remember, however, that you are writing words that will be spoken aloud. Choose your vocabulary and the sentence length accordingly.

11. *Make such notes as will help you in the pulpit.* Some preachers take the full manuscript into the pulpit, underlining or highlighting key points, but not reading the manuscript word for word.

12. *Practice preaching the sermon aloud*—perhaps in the empty church or in your study or home. The church is the preferred place because you can imagine the people sitting there and preach your sermon to them.

If you were preaching a sermon not as dependent upon Scripture, the preparation process would differ, but the steps could be somewhat similar. For example, in the life situation sermon, you need to analyze the situation or problem and then define the Christian goal or standard for this area of life. You would then consider Christian resources that could be brought to bear upon the situation.

How is the busy pastor to complete all of these steps every week? Dr. James Armstrong, a noted preacher and a former bishop of the United Methodist Church, proposed this weekly schedule for sermon preparation in a seminar on preaching at The Iliff School of Theology.

Monday. Determine the scripture basis and theme for the sermon. State in one sentence the intent of the sermon. Ask yourself, What function is this sermon to perform? What response do I expect from those who hear it?

Tuesday. Take the day off. The Holy Spirit can work as the theme (idea) of the sermon is simmering.

Wednesday. Prepare the first draft in skeletal (outline) form.[13]

Thursday. Flesh out the outline, keeping in mind that ideas ought to be logical and sequential. Determine appropriate places to fit in illustrations. Make certain there is depth to your sermon. Ask if this sermon is really meeting the needs of the people. You should have the gospel and a word of hope in every sermon. People are battered and hurting.

Friday. Write the sermon. Do it in one setting. Have fun as you write it out and recall what a privilege it is to speak to a group of people about important matters. Keep the people of your congregation in mind as you write, but never betray a confidence.

Saturday (or Friday night). Give the sermon a reading or two, and edit if necessary. Prepare to deliver the sermon.

Sunday. Get up early and spend some time going over the sermon, especially the last part (the conclusion). Immerse yourself in the sermon. Do not memorize but relive it.

Delivering the Sermon

A sermon is prepared so it can be presented orally to a group of people. One could say that a sermon is not really a sermon until it is preached. The delivery of the sermon is of crucial importance in determining whether real communication takes place. A well-written manuscript can fail to communicate if the delivery of the message is weak and ineffective.

Very few persons can read a manuscript word for word and communicate well. When the sermon is read, eye contact is minimal, and that is more of a problem than it once was. As Michael Rogness points out, "Today's listeners are shaped by television." He notes that "people come to church accustomed to direct eye to eye contact on television, and they sense by TV instinct when the pastor's attention is focused on the manuscript." A further implication is that many preachers need to spend more time preparing for the delivery of their sermon than was true in the past. Rogness says that he personally finds "it necessary to go through the sermon out loud at least three times before I can give it without reading."[14]

If eye contact is sustained, the delivery is likely to be more forceful, direct, and vital. The pattern of speaking will vary in a natural way, rather than being a monotonous "no higher, no lower, no faster, no slower." Important points will receive appropriate emphasis and bodily movements will reinforce the message rather than detract from it. The outcome should be that the preacher stays in vital relationship to the things being said and thus holds the attention of the people.

Preaching is one of the most difficult tasks a minister is asked to perform. No one is fully adequate for the task. But God somehow takes our thoughts and words and transforms them into a message that can challenge or comfort those who hear it.

10

Christian Education

The ministry of Jesus was one of teaching, as well as preaching and healing. Matthew's Gospel says that Jesus "went about all Galilee teaching in their synagogues and preaching the gospel of the kingdom and healing every disease and every infirmity among the people" (Matt. 4:23). Similar statements are made in Matthew 9:35 and Matthew 13:53.

Notice that teaching is the first activity mentioned in this description of the threefold nature of the ministry of Jesus. In Matthew 5 we read those now-familiar statements known as the Beatitudes. Following the Beatitudes, Jesus makes a number of startling statements that follow a specific pattern, beginning with, "You have heard it said . . . ," and continuing with, "but I say to you." Jesus' hearers sensed freshness, challenge, and authority in his teaching. His words surprised them. We are told in Matthew 7:28 "When Jesus finished these sayings, the crowds were astonished at his teaching, for he taught them as one who had authority, and not as their scribes."

Jesus taught whenever and wherever there were persons, whether on a street corner, a hillside, or a lake shore. While not the designated leader of a synagogue, Jesus was clearly seen as a teacher. He was addressed as "teacher" by scribes (Matt. 8:18) and by Pharisees (Matt. 9:11). Jesus was a teacher to the twelve men he had chosen as his closest followers. Matthew 11:1 says that "when Jesus had finished instructing his twelve disciples, he went on from there to teach and preach in their cities."

His method of teaching was varied. Sometimes he taught in a brief conversation with one person, while at other times he made a more extended address to a large crowd. He taught by actions as well as words. Sometimes an act of healing was followed by a brief word of explanation or instruction.

One of his most effective ways of teaching was through parables. Matthew 13:3 says that Jesus "told them many things in parables." Perhaps the best definition of a parable is that it is "an earthly story with a heavenly meaning." Jesus was obviously a master storyteller. He took the ordinary, everyday experiences of the people of his day and used them in a story that held their attention, captured their imagination, and taught them an important truth.

The Role of the Pastor in Christian Education

Like the disciples whom Jesus called to share in his ministry, we today are called to continue the ministry of teaching, preaching, and healing. In this chapter we focus our attention on the ministry of teaching, or as it is sometimes described, Christian education.

Churches of the Reformed tradition have always recognized that the teaching function of the pastor is crucial to the continuing health and welfare of any congregation. The minister is designated as the teaching elder of the congregation. In the "Pastoral Development Inventory" prepared by the Vocation Agency of the United Presbyterian Church in the U.S.A., one of the designated roles of the minister is that of "Coordinator of Church Education." As the document states, "Education has historically enjoyed a high priority in the church. In the Reformed tradition the pastor is looked on as the resident theologian and teacher in the parish. The teaching ministry is essential to the continued health and growth of the church."[1]

Although denominations not in the Reformed tradition may use other terminology to describe the teaching function of the pastor, all recognize its importance. Orthodox and Roman Catholic Christians speak of "the teaching authority of the Church," giving instruction in the faith an institutional character. "Rabbi" is still the official title of the leader of a Jewish synagogue or congregation.

In chapter 5 on reflecting, we emphasized the importance of the pastor's role in helping people think theologically about life. One of the minister's tasks is to teach the faith, leading to spiritual formation and understanding. A minister is expected to be an interpreter—an interpreter of religious truth and of life experience. Reflection is a part of this process of interpretation.

If indeed the pastor is acknowledged to be the coordinator of Christian education in the congregation, as the Presbyterian document mentioned earlier proposes, the pastor has overall responsibility to see that an effective program of religious education is planned and implemented. This obviously does not mean that the minister does it all alone. That would be undesirable even if it were possible. Rather, the pastor works with the other leaders of the church to make sure an effective Christian education program is carried out.

Unfortunately, some clergy see the educational program of the church as something that can be shoved off onto someone else, relieving the pastor of all responsibility. However, even if someone else, such as a Church school superintendent or a paid staff member is designated to take charge of the program, the pastor should not exempt herself or himself from this important aspect of the life of the church.

The minister needs to be involved in goal setting, securing and training leaders, developing and evaluating specific programs, and providing adequate financial support for the program. Also, the minister should be willing to accept certain specific teaching responsibilities. The size of the congregation, the number of paid staff, the number of worship services, are all variables that need to be considered when the pastor's specific responsibilities are determined. For example, the pastor serving a two- or three-point charge will need to work hard at being involved in the Christian education program of the parish. The pastor may arrange for an occasional lay speaker or guest preacher so that the pastor can be included in the Sunday morning educational activities. In the case of a larger congregation with a paid professional in charge of the Christian education program, the senior minister will still want to be kept informed of the plans and activities of the educational program, and also have some direct involvement, as well.

If Sunday morning is too crowded with the responsibilities of worship leadership and preaching, the pastor can teach at other times. There can be a midweek Bible study or a short-term course on a specific topic. Teaching the catechism classes is a good opportunity to get to know the children of the church. It is also important for the pastor to provide the leadership for church membership instruction classes for adults. This personal contact between pastor and new members helps the new members feel a sense of belonging. The pastor also benefits by knowing these persons and thus is able to provide more effective pastoral care, should it be needed in the future.

Components of an Effective Program

In a document entitled "The Nature and Mission of the Church," the Division of Ordained Ministry of the United Methodist Church suggests that Christian education should be seen as a nurturing ministry. Quoting from the *Discipline* of this denomination, the document suggests that the effective congregation will have a church school that

> provides a variety of settings and resources for all persons, children, youth and adults—to explore the meanings of the Christian faith in all its dimensions, to discover and appropriate to themselves those meanings which are relevant for their lives and society, and to assume personal responsibility for expressing those meanings in all their relationships. Through such experiences persons will be encouraged to commit themselves to Christ and to unite with the Christian community through membership in a local church.[2]

This quotation is an example of the kind of purpose statement a congregation needs to prepare for its Christian education program. This purpose statement then leads to the establishment of more specific objectives and action goals and also is an important tool in the evaluation process.

Notice how broad the purpose statement is, referring to a "variety of settings and resources for all persons." Too often the church thinks of Christian education in a limited way. The classes for children and youth that take place on Sunday morning may be the only activities that come to mind for some people when they think of Christian education. Fortunately, many congregations have a much broader understanding of Christian education, with a myriad of activities taking place in the name of Christian education.

Also note the reference at the end to persons being encouraged to "commit themselves to Christ and to unite with the Christian community through membership in a local church." We sometimes forget the important connection between education and evangelism. Children are often introduced to the church in a nursery class, and then in more advanced Sunday church school classes they are provided with greater knowledge of what it means to be a Christian. They may attend a catechism or confirmation class that specifically prepares them for church membership. At an appropriate time they are invited officially to join the church. The exact way in which all this happens varies from one denomination to another, but the role of education in this process should not be minimized.

Likewise, adults who visit a church may come initially to attend a worship service and hear a preacher. However, if that is their only involvement in the life of the congregation, their membership roots may be shallow. They are more likely to become committed members if they become part of a small study or fellowship group. Through these more in-depth relationships, they develop a sense of Christian community, while at the same time gaining knowledge about what it means to be a Christian.

Participation in a church membership class provides the specific preparation they need to enter fully into membership in the congregation. If the small group educational experience does not precede the act of joining the church, every attempt should be made to see that it happens after people join the church. This assimilation needs to take place if people are to remain active.

Leadership

Most congregations, unless they are extremely small membership churches, will have a committee with major responsibility for the Christian education program of the church. In the small membership church, there may simply be one committee or council or board that deals with a variety of program areas in the life of the congregation.

Regardless of how this committee is structured or what its portfolio of responsibilities are, the pastor needs to work closely with this group. Usually, the pastor is an ex-officio member of the group. This does not mean that the minister dominates the group and vetoes any decision she or he does not like. Rather, the pastor is the resource person, the consultant, who assists the group with helpful information and suggestions. The minister may have to do some leadership training with the group or arrange to have them participate in a Christian education training program conducted by someone else.

This committee needs to develop a comprehensive purpose statement and then work out objectives and goals. The committee needs to be clear about its role and its relationship to the pastor, to other decision making bodies in the congregation, and to the persons who do the actual teaching. In a large congregation the committee may need to designate subcommittee chairpersons who will work with the various age levels represented in the congregation. Larger denominations usually provide guidelines for the various program areas of the congregation. The pastor should make certain that such resources are made available to the committee.

The recruitment, training, and support of the teachers or leaders of the Christian education program is crucial to the success of the program. Not everyone willing to teach is qualified or suited to teach. The Christian education committee should have specific criteria by which teachers are selected. A personal interview of the prospective teacher by one or more persons might be appropriate, especially if the person is relatively new in the congregation or has never taught before. This screening process is especially important for persons who will be working with children and youth. While obtaining the needed teachers by such a process may be difficult, think of the potential for negative consequences if the wrong person is allowed to teach. We have become aware of the possibility that persons in positions of trust might betray that trust.

When specific people are invited to teach, the demands of the position need to be recognized, but training can be offered and the personal satisfaction rewards of the position can be noted. The person can be asked to serve as an assistant to another teacher before taking sole responsibility for a class. There can be a probationary period agreed on, after which the teacher and committee can decide whether the teacher should continue and for how long. Team teaching may be one way to make the experience easier and more enjoyable for the teachers, allowing one of them to be gone occasionally. Even though this arrangement requires more persons, more persons are likely to say yes when the responsibility will be shared. Times of fellowship and recognition should be arranged on a regular basis. Some churches include in their Sunday morning worship an annual service of installation for those who serve in the educational program of the congregation.

Curriculum

In a personal interview Dr. Clarence Snelling, professor of teaching ministries at The Iliff School of Theology, stated that "the job of Christian Education in the twenty-first century is helping a congregation create the appropriate religious language that expresses their religious experience." That task is not new. Both John and Charles Wesley did it, and numerous other examples could be cited, going back even to the letters of Paul to the churches.

We sometimes presume that religious language is already in place, and that in Christian education all we have to do is recite the language or state the definitions. However, instead of simply imparting information, we need to help people recognize the forms of their own religious life and reflect on their experiences in the light of their religious faith and understanding. Dr. Snelling says that "the primary task of Christian education is nurturing the imagination of children, youth, and adults."

Keeping in mind its purpose statement, the leadership of a congregation must strive to develop a comprehensive Christian education program that will be inviting to the whole range of persons potentially available for participation. Notice the words "potentially available." Too often a church attends only to those presently participating in its Christian education program. The church, however, needs to ask itself whether there are persons not presently involved in the Christian education program who have needs the church could meet. This can be done by considering the various age levels and the programs presently available for persons in that age level.

Children and youth are often seen as the primary focus of the Christian education program of the congregation. That is appropriate, but there may be persons in these age groups who are unintentionally excluded. For example, transportation may be a problem for some children. Parents may be uninterested, or unemployed, or have some other reason they cannot bring their children to the educational and fellowship activities of the church. In such situations, some churches provide vans or busses; some arrange car pools or get volunteers to drive their own cars.

There may also be children who are mentally retarded or have other special needs. Perhaps a class for these children with special needs can be established with leadership provided by unpaid volunteers from the church. Another possibility is a summer program, perhaps with financial underwriting from local businesses, so a professionally trained teacher can be hired. Each church needs to find out what unmet needs exist in the community and then determine what it can do to meet those needs. Need-based Christian education is likely to be the most successful.

One of the exciting things happening in Christian education today is the increased interest in adult education. Adults are taking continuing education classes of all kinds, often just out of curiosity or for personal enrichment. Sunday morning is still the traditional time for such classes in the church, but other times of the week are also being utilized. Three kinds of curriculum seem to be most commonly emphasized in adult Christian education today.

1. *Basic to all Christian education is Bible study.* Many persons, including church members, are biblically illiterate. They would find it difficult to tell whether a particular book of the Bible is in the Old Testament (Hebrew Bible) or the New Testament. They may even think Sodom and Gomorrah were two lovers, vaguely recall that there is a story in the Bible about a boy who "loafs and fishes."

The Bethel Bible Study program, begun many years ago by a Lutheran congregation in Madison, Wisconsin, has been used effectively in numerous congregations. It has been received appreciatively by many people who were willing to make a long-term commitment to in-depth, serious, interesting Bible study. Other mainline denominations have recently produced similar Bible study programs, such as the Discipleship program of the United Methodist Church.

Not all persons will commit to a long-term Bible study but would be interested in a shorter study program, perhaps one that examines one or more specific books of the Bible. This class might meet during the week rather than on Sunday, and it might be taught by the pastor. Some congregations offer the same course of study during the day and again in the evening. Older people or anyone not employed during the day may prefer the daytime meeting.

2. *A class can be offered on a specific topic for a stated period of time.* Again, this can be offered either on Sunday morning or at some other time. Some large congregations will have several such classes offered on Sunday morning on different topics. For example, a class on Christian parenting may be offered for parents of young children, while another class may deal with medical ethics and the Christian faith. Still another may consider the denomination's heritage. People know how often the class will meet, and they are committed to attend the class only for that length of time. Courses such as these are often taught by outside resource persons or by lay members of the congregation who have special knowledge and interest in a particular topic. If a nonmember is the instructor, the church will likely need to budget for an honorarium. The cost can be covered in the Christian education budget, or the church may charge a nominal fee or take up a freewill offering each time the class meets.

These classes on a specific topic often use as a resource books from one of the religious publishers or from a supplier of church school curriculum materials. Audiovisuals of all kinds are available and may allow a study group to meet without an expert on the topic to serve as the leader or resource person.

3. *The adult forum has become an increasingly popular approach to adult Christian education.* Usually this program is offered on Sunday morning during the traditional Sunday school time. A small committee chooses topics and speakers. Sometimes one speaker will lead the group for several consecutive Sundays. One person from the committee serves as the convener and facilitator for the program, introducing the speaker and the topic and adjourning each session.

This kind of program works particularly well if the church is located in a large city where a variety of resource persons are readily available. Persons involved in other helping professions, such as pastoral counselors, medical doctors, social workers, and directors of programs for the poor and homeless, are often invited in to speak. International exchange students, teachers with knowledge of a topic or area of the world currently in the news can be interesting and informative resource persons. People in the congregation who have particularly interesting experiences, work, or hobbies may also be invited.

Even if the congregation is not located in a metropolitan area, there still may be interesting speakers available. If planners do not consider them appropriate for a Sunday morning class, such speakers might be asked to lead programs for various groups in the church at other times.

Although there is usually a core group of loyal persons who attend all or most of the adult forum sessions, it is generally understood that people may choose to come or not to come, depending upon the topic and speaker. Thus attendance can vary considerably. Because the topic and speaker are constantly changing, good publicity is vital. The schedule should provide at least a three month's listing of topics and speakers. While many of the speakers may not require an honorarium, that needs to be discussed with the speaker when the invitation to speak is given. This program needs to have a budget for some honoraria. Often a freewill offering is taken at each forum session, but the amount received may not be adequate to cover all costs.

Time and Space

The time and place a group meets are important factors in the success of a group. Usually the members of the group will have strong opinions about the best meeting time for the group. Conflict may develop and some members or potential members may not participate because of the meeting time.

Each congregation must determine what kind of a schedule is possible and what is desirable. At times, those two criteria may be opposed to one another. Sunday morning can be a particular problem if a pastor serves two or more congregations. The customary solution is for one congregation to have an early worship service followed by the church school. The other congregation will begin its Sunday morning program with church school and the worship service will follow. Some such yoked parishes reverse the format annually in order to be fair. Other parishes prefer to keep the same schedule indefinitely.

One issue that arises in some congregations is whether to have the Sunday church school meet at the same time the worship service is taking place. Some parents like this arrangement because it requires less of their time on Sunday morning. Some worshipers probably like it, even if they do not have children in Sunday church school, because they do not have to "put up" with disruptive children in the worship service. Some pastors may like the fact that they are preaching only to adults and can plan their sermons accordingly.

However, some disadvantages are that children and youth who are in church school cannot attend worship with their parents. If the children do attend worship, then they cannot participate in the church school program. Also, adults who are the teachers are excluded from worship with the congregation, and adults who attend worship are excluded from participation in the Sunday morning adult education program. Even if a class is offered for adults before or after worship, those who have children will need to leave with their children. Some churches have children present for the first part of the service, and then the children leave for junior church, choir practice, or other activities.

These problems are alleviated to some extent if the church has more than one worship service on Sunday morning and church school is scheduled only during one of the two services. However, this schedule is still likely to reduce the participation of children in worship and the participation of adults in education. A much better option is to schedule the church school between the two worship services. Each church needs to determine what best fits the desires and needs of its community and its members.

Space is another consideration that is sometimes related to schedule. Limited worship space may require multiple worship services in a growing congregation. That in turn may affect the schedule for education. Some churches have two Sunday school sessions on a Sunday morning because of limited space. Parking space may affect scheduling.

Funds are always limited when it comes to constructing facilities for worship, education, and fellowship, but space is influential in determining our feelings and our readiness to learn. The situation may be better for congregations that have newer buildings, but many congregations still hold classes in unattractive, poorly lighted basements, and even boiler rooms. Such arrangements suffer from the contrast with public school facilities that these same children attend during the week.

The Christian education program of any local church deserves the best possible space that can be provided. As new buildings are built or remodeling takes place, bring in consultants, visit other educational facilities, and try not to shortchange this important aspect of the program of the church.

Places other than the church building itself can sometimes be used as activity centers or meeting places. The church might have a playground area for small children, an outdoor worship area, even an area where volleyball or other games can be played. Summer allows for field trips and meetings to take place outdoors. Homes and yards of members of a group can provide a delightful change of scenery. Parks and public recreation areas can sometimes be utilized for special events. Be imaginative in your thinking about the use of space, both inside and outside your building.

Education is tremendously important in the life of the church and the community. At the conclusion of a lecture, Paul Tillich, a German-born theologian, was asked, "How could the Germans do what they did to the Jews?" The reference, of course, was to the Holocaust. There was a shocked silence in the auditorium as the audience waited for Dr. Tillich's answer to this very bold and embarrassing question. Dr. Tillich paused briefly, and then said very simply and quietly, "They forgot the meaning of their symbols."

What a simple and yet profound answer to an enormous question. But what wisdom it suggests. Christian education helps us remember our symbols, the values by which we as individuals and as a society must live if civilization is to continue to exist.

11

Evangelism

Faith Church had been in the same little building in the same big city for many years. The congregation had dwindled in size but still managed to survive. Unable to afford a full-time pastor, the congregation was forced to hire a student from the nearby theological seminary to be their part-time pastor. Pastor Dan, their present student pastor, was a doctoral student at the seminary. He was ordained and had prior pastoral experience. In spite of the negatives in the situation, he was enthusiastic about the potential of the church. He was determined to bring some new vitality to the congregation.

One Sunday, as he greeted the congregation after worship, Pastor Dan engaged a young woman visitor in conversation, learning her name (Sally) and welcoming her. Then he asked, "How did you happen to visit our church this morning?"

She replied, "Oh, I just live a few houses from the church and I walk by your church every day to and from the bus stop. I haven't been going to church anywhere for quite a while and often thought about visiting this church but never did. I guess what finally made me decide to come was the signboard out in front."

"What was it about the signboard that motivated you?" asked the pastor.

"Well," said Sally, "that signboard had stayed the same ever since I moved here. It never changed. Then about two months ago I noticed something different. The name of the pastor was changed and each week there was a different sermon title posted. I decided something must be happening at the church and it made me curious enough to want to visit."

The pastor thanked Sally for coming and expressed the hope that she would return next Sunday. He made certain that she had filled out a visitor's card, with name, address, and telephone number.

What can we learn about evangelism from this little scenario about Faith Church?

1. *The role of the pastor in evangelism is critical.* Only after Pastor Dan arrived did the sign outside the church get changed. He had also convinced the trustees to do some exterior painting to give the church a fresh look. He made sure the interior of the church was clean and neat and made arrangements to have the grass mowed regularly and the shrubbery trimmed. It was Pastor Dan who talked with Sally at the conclusion of the service. Perhaps members of the congregation talked with her as well, but we do not know that.

2. *The appearance of the building and grounds can influence persons positively or negatively.* A neat, well cared for building, a nicely landscaped yard, and adequate parking will be attractive to potential visitors. The building itself can be an advertisement.

3. *The church should know its neighbors.* Sally had lived near the church for some time but had never visited the church. Nor, apparently, had anyone from the church ever invited her.

4. *Sally came as a visitor to the Sunday morning worship service.* As Patrick Keifert points out in his book *Welcoming the Stranger,* "Unlike the pattern in the three decades after World War II, when people typically sought out pastors or congregational members before they came to church, most unchurched visitors in the 1980s made their first formal contacts with the institutional church as unannounced visitors to 'check out' Sunday morning worship services."[1] Sunday morning worship is an evangelistic opportunity that should not be ignored.

5. *A follow-up to Sally's visit was planned but apparently only by the pastor.* There is a strong correlation between follow-up contact with visitors, in person or by phone, and the continuing involvement of visitors in the life of the congregation. Lay people are sometimes more effective in making the initial call than the pastor.

6. *Sally may be single and want to know, "What other programs does this church offer that will be of interest to me?"* Single young adults are generally few in numbers, especially in smaller churches, yet they want to relate to other single young adults.

7. *The future of Faith Church is precarious.* It is primarily a congregation of older people, most of whom do not live in the neighborhood. The church has limited off-street parking. Their student pastor will likely leave as soon as his degree is received. The only possibility for the survival of the congregation is to bring in people from the neighborhood. If these neighborhood people become part of the church, the church will change. In fact, the church will probably need to change before any substantial number of neighborhood people will participate.

8. *The program of evangelism will differ from church to church.* Each congregation needs to determine its identity, know its neighborhood, and plan its program. How evangelism is carried out in Faith Church will vary considerably from the program in a church located in a rapidly growing, affluent suburb.

Definitions of Evangelism

Our consideration of Faith Church has provided us with some important insights about evangelism. However, we have not yet defined the word "evangelism." Some pastors believe that everything done in and by the church is evangelism. Others define evangelism too narrowly, equating it with revivalism or thinking of it as only one kind of personal experience. By thinking of evangelism as a private religious experience, some people separate evangelism totally from social consciousness and action.

Evangelism is a form of the word *evangel,* which literally means "good news." Therefore, evangelism is to proclaim the good news. The Foundation for Evangelism of the United Methodist Church expands the meaning: "Evangelism is offering Christ by word and deed, to the end that persons may *experience* God's forgiveness, *find acceptance* in the Christian fellowship and *become involved* in Christ's continuing mission in the world."[2] In his book *The Pastor Evangelist in the Parish,* Richard Stoll Armstrong explains, "Evangelism is proclaiming in word and deed the good news of the kingdom of God, and calling people to repentance, to personal faith in Jesus Christ as Lord and Savior, to active membership in the church, and to obedient service in the world."[3]

Notice how similar these two definitions of evangelism are. Both definitions use the phrase "word and deed," emphasizing that evangelism involves not only what we say but also what we do. Another similarity is the comprehensive nature of these definitions. No wonder Dr. Armstrong says, "Evangelism is not just one thing among many that a pastor does. It is the heart of *everything* a pastor does!"[4]

However, we dare not assume, therefore, that evangelism does not need any special focus of attention. Evangelism needs to be seen as a central emphasis of the church deserving of specific leadership, goals, and programs. If understood in a comprehensive way, as these definitions suggest, evangelism can be an integrating factor in the total practice of ministry. However, that integration will not take place unless the pastor and congregation are intentional about it.

Although evangelism is the proclamation of *good* news, it has a negative connotation for some people. The task of the pastor is to deal with such negative images so the church can develop a positive program of evangelism.

The Need for Evangelism

Statistics confirm what denominational leaders and local church pastors have known for quite some time—membership is declining in mainline denominations. One researcher, George Barna, believes that the decline in membership of mainline Protestant denominations indicates how poorly most churches are responding to the cultural transition taking place in our society. According to Mr. Barna, "Churches tell people, you must play by our rules. But people today say, I don't have to play by your rules. I'll go where my needs are met."[5] Barna thinks churches need to use more "up-to-date methodology to transmit their theology" without compromising the gospel.

Much has been said and written about that group of people born between 1946 and 1964, often referred to as the baby boomers. Tex Sample describes baby boomers in *U.S. Lifestyles and Mainline Churches.* He notes that during this eighteen year period, 76.4 million babies were born in this nation, the largest generation in United States history. These baby boomers constitute nearly one in three persons in our society.[6] He says the baby boomers represent a shift in values from self-denial to self-fulfillment. Sample credits Daniel Yankelovich for identifying three ingredients in this ethic. One is that life itself is "intrinsically valuable" and therefore not to be denied for the sake of something else. Second, "life is to be creatively and emotionally expressive."[7] Phrases like "Let it all hang out" or "Do it now" are indicative of this attitude. A third ingredient of the self-fulfillment attitude is an emphasis on affluence. When asked what they want in life, the baby boomers most committed to the value of self-fulfillment are likely to say "more."[8] Sample points out that "the generation missing from the mainline churches is this group of young adults in their twenties, thirties and forties," and "the more strongly one holds to an ethic of self-fulfillment, the less likely one is to belong to the church."[9] The result is that churches filled with people who hold to a self-denial ethic have difficulty attracting the baby boomers.

Sample goes on to describe this generation of baby boomers in terms of the cultural left, the cultural right, and the cultural middle. The mainline churches have "lost the baby boomers of the cultural left and middle in massive numbers," says Sample.[10] On the other hand, the conservative churches have continued to grow because baby boomers of the cultural right have kept up their relationship to the church. Sample's book continues by suggesting ministry strategies for reaching each of these cultural groups.

Even more recent research in regard to baby boomers and religion has been carried out by Wade Clark Roof, a sociologist at the University of California at Santa Barbara. Using Roof's findings, an article in *Time* in April 1993 reports that about a third (of the baby boomers) have never strayed from the church. Another one-fourth of boomers are defectors who have returned to religious practice—at least for now. "However, 'the returnees' are still vastly outnumbered by the 42% of baby boomers who remain dropouts from formal religion."[11] Although the dropouts interviewed by Roof remain dropouts, most of them felt it was important for their children to have religious instruction. When the dropouts were asked what might bring them back into the church they said that two such events would be "having children and facing at midlife a personal or career crisis that reminds (them) of the need for moorings."[12]

Roof's research seems to support the strong probability that a pattern of the past will continue—some young people drop out of church activities in their late teens and do not return to the church until they marry and have children old enough to receive religious training. Churches need to be alert to this possibility and to be ready to offer a strong program of Christian education for children, as well as group activities for the parents. Furthermore, the possibility of a personal or career crisis motivating people to seek out the church indicates the importance of the church letting it be known that pastoral care and counseling are available.

Another significant finding by Roof is the growth of what he calls "believers but not belongers." They are likely to seek out the church in time of need. They may even visit a church occasionally, especially at Christmas and Easter.

Reaching the Baby Boomers

Learning about the characteristics of the baby boomers is an important first step in designing a program of evangelism to enable the local church to reach these people with the gospel. The Rev. Robert Schuller, pastor of the Crystal Cathedral in Garden Grove, California, has some advice for mainline Protestant denominations that keep showing a net loss in membership: "Quit talking about social ethics in Sunday services and address instead psychological hurts and needs."[13] Schuller's formula is a simple one. "Find a need and fill it. Find a hurt and heal it." However, by itself this formula does not constitute an adequate prescription for a program of evangelism. (In fairness to Dr. Schuller, I do not think he intended it as such.)

According to William Easum, "In order to minister to this diverse, changing world of choices, mainstream Protestant churches need to make basic changes in leadership skills, the quality and scope of ministry, and the method of preaching and worship."[14] Easum believes what needs to change is "the manner in which pastors and laity proclaim, package, market and give leadership to the Good News." The goal of these changes is "to move Baby Boomers from the pursuit of self-centered self-fulfillment to the biblical understanding of self-fulfillment through self-denial."[15]

In order to reach the baby boomers, Easum says that pastors and laity must make a fundamental change in attitude, to "look outward to the needs of others rather than centering our thoughts on ourselves."[16] Easum's counsel recalls a biblical injunction, Paul's words to the church at Philippi: "Do nothing from selfishness or conceit but in humility count others better than yourselves. Let each of you look not only to your own interests but also to the interests of others" (Philippians 2:3-4).

We need to recognize that sometimes our motives for engaging in evangelism are not entirely altruistic. When we reach out to the unchurched, our concern may be to increase the membership to get more people to help pay off the mortgage or even to enhance the reputation of the pastor. Or do we reach out to the unchurched because we care deeply about others and want to share the good news in response to the command of Christ?

In *Understanding Church Growth*, Donald McGavran states that "evangelism intends the redemption of individuals and the multiplication of Christ's churches. Concern for evangelism and church growth is an essential part of the Christian faith and an irreplaceable part of the work of the church."[17] But church growth proponents point out, "church growth is much wider and deeper than adding names to church rolls. It delves into how persons and peoples become genuinely Christian and revolutionize and bless the cultures and populations in the midst of which God has placed them."[18]

A Program of Evangelism

In *Effective Evangelism* George Sweazey describes evangelism as a series of connected steps, with the goal being "to bring people, through Jesus Christ, to walk with God."[19] He expresses each of these steps in one word beginning with the letter "c." The four steps are contact, cultivation, commitment, and conservation. These steps provide a useful outline for describing a comprehensive program of evangelism.

Contact

Somehow the church has to locate and make contact with unchurched people who may be prospects for membership. One way to discover how many people living in the immediate area around the church might be prospects is to conduct a *religious census* of the neighborhood.

Some churches *advertise* in a local newspaper. In small communities with a weekly newspaper, church notices are often carried free of charge. Make certain that the information is correct. Human interest stories about persons or programs of the church are usually welcomed by newspapers. Talk with the appropriate editor or reporter to learn about their policies and deadlines. If you prepare a good news release so that the paper does not have to spend a lot of time rewriting it, the chances are much better that it will be printed. Also, in small communities, a local radio station may carry public service announcements without charge, or advertising time can be purchased for a nominal cost. Be sure the telephone yellow pages carry information about the church, including the schedule of church school and worship.

The building itself can be a good advertisement, encouraging people to want to come inside (remember Faith Church). Good signs, with correct, up-to-date information are important. Night lighting can be effective; use either exterior lighting and/or interior lighting that shows the beauty of a stained glass window. Making the building available to not-for-profit neighborhood groups, such as a chapter of AARP (American Association of Retired Persons), for no charge or only a token charge is another way to acquaint people with the church and meet a need in the community.

A major reason why people come to visit a church is that *somebody invited them.* Members of the congregation need to be reminded that during the course of a week they will interact with many people, most of whom the pastor does not know and will never meet. Some of these people are not attending any church and if invited might attend the church to which they have been invited.

Activities in addition to Sunday worship can be a means of attracting people to the church. Herb Miller, in *How To Build the Magnetic Church,*[20] tells of a pastor who called on a couple for six years. The people were always pleasant and said they planned to attend the church but never did. Then one day a church member who was a friend of the husband invited him to play on the church softball team. The man was an excellent pitcher and helped the team begin to win games. In a few weeks the family began attending worship. Three months later they joined the church, and three years later the man was elected to chair the administrative board of the church. Sports such as softball, bowling, volleyball, and basketball have proved to be effective ways of getting outsiders involved and interested in the church. Some of these activities, and others with more appeal to women, can be an important part of the outreach program of the church.

Cultivation

We already know that the first real contact with the church is likely to be a visit to a Sunday morning worship service to check out the church (recall Faith Church). What the visitor experiences on that first visit will help determine whether the visitor returns.

In a workshop on evangelism Herb Miller stated five reasons people keep coming back: (1) friendliness, (2) positive, upbeat worship, (3) a pastor to whom they can relate, (4) a doctrinal position that makes sense to them, and (5) broad programming that will meet their needs.

Note that the number one reason is "friendliness." Some churches think of themselves as very friendly, but the members are friendly only to one another. However, recall the incident recorded in Luke 5. A paralyzed man was brought to Jesus to be healed, but the people in the room where Jesus was speaking were crowded so closely around Jesus there was no way for the paralyzed man to be brought to Jesus. The men who brought the paralytic had to go up on the roof and lower the man through the tiles so he could be healed (Luke 5:18-20). This incident reminds us that those closest to Jesus can form such a tightly knit group that the outsider, the stranger, finds it almost impossible to break into the group and be accepted.

The friendly greeting of visitors should be the responsibility of all members, but specific persons need to be assigned that responsibility. Having designated greeters at the entrances to the building does not preclude other members from welcoming visitors. In some large churches, people may not know who is a visitor. In that case the church needs to have some way of identifying visitors, perhaps by giving them a flower or a ribbon to wear. Having a fellowship time after the worship service, or between services if there is more than one, is a way of encouraging friendliness. Some churches have name tags members are asked to wear so that people get to know each other by name. A picture directory of the church is another way to get people acquainted with one another.

Finding out who the visitors are is extremely important so that follow-up can be made. Having visitors sign a guest book is not very effective because some visitors do not sign, or the information is incomplete. Many churches use a "ritual of friendship" pad in their worship services. At a designated time in the service, pads are distributed by the ushers to the outside person in each pew. People are asked to write names, addresses, and phone numbers and then pass the pad along to the next person. When the pad reaches the inside aisle, it is passed back to the other end. This allows people to find out who is seated in that pew. Visitors are easily identified, and after the service has ended people can greet one another and get acquainted. The ritual of friendship not only identifies visitors and encourages friendliness, but also provides information about the attendance of members. Continuous absence of a member for several Sundays may indicate a problem and suggest the need for a pastoral contact.

The information on the registration sheets needs to be compiled as soon as possible, with immediate attention focused on local visitors. (Out-of-town visitors can be mailed a note later in the week thanking them for visiting the church.) The reason for quickly compiling visitor information is so that visits can be made to the homes of local visitors. Miller says that "no single factor makes a greater difference in improving annual membership additions than an immediate visit to the homes of first-time worshipers." Miller claims that "when laypersons make fifteen minute visits to the home of first-time worship visitors within thirty-six hours, 85 percent of them return the following week. Make this home visit within seventy-two hours and 60 percent of them return. Make it seven days later, and 15 percent will return. The pastor making this call, rather than laypersons, cuts each result in half."[21]

These statistics underscore the importance of having trained lay visitors who will commit themselves to this ministry of visitation evangelism. The size of the congregation and the anticipated number of visitors will help determine how many people are needed for this ministry. Individuals or couples can be asked to serve for a year. Individuals need not be members of the evangelism committee.

The visitation team will need some training, which the pastor should be able to provide. Herb Miller's book, as well as other books, films, and denominational materials are available as training resources. The group will want to meet periodically for mutual support and fellowship, as well as education.

Members of the visitation team can remain for a few minutes after worship and meet to review the registration pads. The names of visitors can be quickly spotted and then team members can decide who will make the visit or visits. The visits should be made no later than Monday evening. A report can be returned the following Sunday.

The question of whether to phone ahead and make an appointment needs to be considered. An advantage of phoning ahead is that the caller can determine if the people will be home. A disadvantage of phoning ahead is that the people may try to dissuade the caller from coming and a phone conversation ensues instead of a personal visit. Because these people have just visited the church and this is a brief call being made by a lay person, it may be better to just "drop by." If the people are not home, a note can be left and a phone call made later.

Attendance at a worship service may be a first point of contact for the visitor, with a call in the home by a layperson being the second contact. During the home visit, the visitor can also describe other opportunities in the church for education and fellowship.

The pastor of a rapidly growing suburban church told me that the "port of entry" for many of their members is the Christian education program of the church. The church places a strong emphasis on adult education. As he put it, "If you go after the children, you get the children. If you go after the adults, you get the family." The church offers a strong program of Christian education for adults as well as for children and youth.

The pastor describes this church as a community of faith. What that means is that "we know one another and we care for one another." He says, "You can't program community but you can provide the atmosphere for community to happen." Some of this community building takes place in the worship service, where there is a time for people to greet one another and for the sharing of concerns. The use of lay liturgists and the participation of a youth choir also help to strengthen community. "Our people are excited about our life together," says the pastor, "and they tell others about the church. Our best advertising is the word-of-mouth advertising of our members."

Commitment

Contact and cultivation should lead to commitment as people become acknowledged followers of Christ and members of the church. Procrastination is a common fault. In one congregation, I was surprised by the number of persons who attended worship quite regularly but who were not members. Some of them were spouses or adult children of persons who were members. Intrigued by these persons, I decided to visit each person or family and talk with them about their relationship to Christ and the church. The results of my visitation surprised me.

Some people told me they were members of the church and I was mistaken in thinking they were not. One man became quite angry that his membership was not listed in the official records of the church. Another person showed me her membership certificate to prove she was a member. I quickly realized that my predecessor minister had not kept good records and had not entrusted that duty to anyone else. Hurt feelings were soothed over and the membership records corrected.

Some people said they still had their membership in a church located in the community where they once lived. They felt a loyalty to their old church and had never taken action to transfer their membership. We talked about the process of transferring membership and a number of them did just that.

Other people had other reasons for not being members. Several said they had not joined when they were younger and just kept putting it off as something they would probably do "someday." These were people with whom I could speak about what it means to be a Christian and why church membership is important.

A number of people surprised me by saying that no one had ever given them a personal invitation to join the church, at least not for a long time. The members of the church thought of them as "friends of the congregation" who knew that they were welcome to join the church at any time. Sometimes people need that special personal invitation, so they know they are really appreciated and wanted.

Each church has to ask the question, "How do we lead people to make a commitment to Christ and the church? Some people will immediately dismiss the question by saying, "Oh, that's the pastor's responsibility," and indeed it is. The pastor should be the chief evangelist in the congregation. But evangelism is the responsibility of the whole congregation, and commitment can happen at various times and places.

In some congregations every worship service includes what is commonly called an "altar call." After the sermon the pastor invites persons who have never accepted Christ as Savior and Lord to come forward and kneel. Other persons, clergy or lay, kneel and pray with them. In some churches, the invitation is to membership in the church, either by confession of faith or transfer. In still other churches, the invitation is to Christian discipleship, which could have a number of interpretations.

Because of what some people view as "emotional manipulation," the altar call has been rejected by many congregations. Instead, persons wanting to know more about what it means to be a Christian or who are considering membership are invited to meet in an adjacent room at the conclusion of the service. A pastor or lay person will meet with them, ascertain their needs, and record pertinent information. A follow-up home visit will then be made by the pastor or a lay visitor.

Sitting down with another person face to face in that person's home is one of the best ways to lead an individual to a commitment to Christ and to the church. The home is safe territory for the person who is being visited. There is time to ask and answer questions. A decision can be made that will be made public later.

The Christian education program of the church is certainly preparation for church membership. Catechism or confirmation classes for
children and youth focus more specifically on the Bible and salvation,
the nature of the church, and what it means to be a Christian. These
classes usually culminate in the children joining the church. Membership instruction for adults is essential, and if the church is large enough,
this is usually conducted as a class rather than on an individual basis.
The pastor needs to be involved in membership instruction at every age
level, even if not responsible for leading every session so the pastor can
begin to establish a pastoral relationship with these people.

Commitment can happen in places other than the church building
and at times other than Sunday morning worship. Church camping
programs have provided the opportunity for many children and youth
to dedicate their lives to Christ. Church retreats and large Christian
gatherings have been the occasion for commitment. Special local
church preaching missions or a religious emphasis week on a college
campus can lead to commitment. Even a radio or television program
based on the gospel can move a person to decision.

Conservation

Interviews of dropouts from congregations of the Reformed Church in
America revealed that the two major reasons people drop out of church
were a feeling that the pastor was not really concerned about them as
persons, and that no one in the congregation provided them with spiritual and psychological support. A similar process of interviewing
dropouts from United Methodist congregations revealed the major
cause to be "anxiety and anger precipitated by relationships among people in the congregation—the pastor, other members and family members."[22] These studies emphasize the importance of people encouraging,
nurturing, and supporting one another. A real or imagined put down by
the pastor or another member can result in a person dropping out of
church. Unless some contact with that person is initiated by the church,
the person may never return.

There are other reasons people drop out of church. According to a
Gallup poll of "unchurched Americans 1988," some people stop coming
to church, not because they are angry at the church or any of its members, but because they want to spend more time doing something else.
That "something else" could be recreation, work, or being with family
and friends. Those who left the church because of negative feelings

"were most likely to cite excessive concern with money and narrow religious beliefs."[23]

People may also drop out of a congregation because they have lost their job, have marital problems, or are dealing with problems with children. They are ashamed to face members of the congregation who know about their problems. How unfortunate when this happens, because these are times the church needs to be the community of faith that surrounds these persons with loving support.

Here are some things a church can do to conserve its new members:

1. *Prepare them for membership through a program of instruction and orientation.* See that they know something about the denominational history, beliefs, and practices. Acquaint them with the congregation they are joining and its leaders. Talk with them about stewardship.

2. *Make the day they join a special occasion.* Put their names in the bulletin. Introduce them to the congregation by sharing some information about them. Give them a flower to wear. Have a reception for them following the worship service when they can be greeted by the other members. Make certain both new and longtime members have name tags.

3. *Assign a sponsoring friend or couple* who will make it their personal responsibility to see that the new members are assimilated into the life of the church. New members may need special support and encouragement for twelve to eighteen months.

4. *Get the new members involved in some activity, group, or program,* in addition to worship, such as choir, an adult fellowship group, Bible study, ushering, a men's club or women's circle, or visiting the elderly.

5. *Consider these new members for leadership roles in the church.* Some churches have term limitations on church leadership positions so vacancies will develop. Find out what the interests and talents of these new members are, and then invite these persons to participate in an appropriate ministry.

6. *Do not overlook evangelism as an activity in which to involve these new members.* These persons, if previously unchurched, will know more unchurched persons than will longtime members. New members, who themselves were attracted to the church, will be enthusiastic when they recommend the church to others.

7. *If after a while new members seem to lose interest and are not participating in the activities of the church, get in touch with them.* Make a personal visit. Find out what is wrong. Get them back on track.

All Christians are called to be witnesses to the gospel and bearers of the good news. Each local church has to determine how evangelism happens in its community, just as each individual needs to figure out what evangelism means for him or her. Evangelism needs to begin with prayer, a focus on persons, and a plan, and it proceeds with patience and persistence.

PART 3

Personal Resources

12

Continuing
Your Education

The framed certificate hanging on the wall states that the minister has received the master of divinity degree from a theological seminary. Can anyone really be a master of divinity? Or is divinity something that eludes us but motivates us to keep growing in our knowledge and ability to be effective ministers? Writing to the church at Philippi, Paul says there is "one thing I do, forgetting what lies behind and straining forward to what lies ahead, I press on toward the goal for the prize of the upward call of God in Christ Jesus" (Philippians 3:12-14).

Paul's attitude is one every minister should emulate. Rather than be complacent about one's faith or knowledge or skill, we need to be open to learning and to growing. A minister's education must not end when he or she receives a degree from a seminary and/or a certificate of ordination. Instead, the minister's education must continue if the minister is to remain effective.

The doctor of ministry degree programs that many seminaries now offer have given numerous clergy the opportunity to continue their theological education in a significant way. However, not all clergy can avail themselves of such a degree program. Instead their continuing education must be self-directed. Interestingly, some religious denominations are requiring their ordained clergy to earn a specified number of continuing education units (CEU'S) in order to remain in good standing. Other professions, such as law, medicine, and teaching have had similar requirements for many years. Religion is now catching up with these other professions by making continuing education a requirement rather than a recommendation.

Setting Continuing Education Goals

If continuing education is going to take place, the pastor will need to take responsibility for it. Continuing education begins by identifying needs to be met and goals to be reached. The pastor may receive feedback from the congregation that indicates an area of weakness or ineffectiveness. Or the pastor may realize something is lacking or not working properly in a particular area of the life of the church. Sometimes an outsider will see something the pastor is not doing well or is not doing at all and can suggest this as an area for continuing education.

The pastor needs to guard against defensiveness and denial if the recommendation is made that some aspect of ministry needs to be strengthened. Instead, the pastor should see this as an opportunity to get support for continuing education and as a chance to learn and grow. Furthermore, the pastor should recognize that this can result in strengthening the total program of the congregation.

When setting goals for continuing education, try to be clear about why you are doing what you plan to do. What is it you hope to learn and what do you expect to do with that knowledge? How will what you have learned impact your ministry and/or the program of the congregation you serve?

Once a need is determined, the pastor should seek information about continuing education opportunities. Where and when are they offered? Or is this need something the pastor can read about on his or her own and then discuss with colleagues?

After the pastor determines the need, sets goals, and learns about resources, participation in a program should follow. The pastor needs to be a full participant, thinking about the implications of the course or program for self and church. The idea is to gain ideas and skills that can be taken back to the church and translated into action. Sometimes a pastor returns home from an exciting conference or educational event brimming with new ideas to try out on the congregation. If the pastor does a poor job of explaining this great new idea and simply imposes it by decree, the response will almost certainly be negative. The pastor has to provide leadership in such a way that people will understand why the change is being made.

Finding Time

The most common excuse given by clergy for not participating more fully in continuing education is lack of time. To some extent this is a valid excuse. The work of a conscientious pastor is never fully done. There is always one more pastoral call that one could make, one more letter that could be written, one more hour that could be spent preparing to lead the worship service. Study time needs to be scheduled, just as family time, sermon preparation time, and meeting times are scheduled. The pastor should not feel guilty when engaged in continuing education. This is a privilege that goes with the heavy demands placed on the pastor. Some sensible balance of time needs to be planned and adhered to as much as possible. Interruptions and exceptions are bound to happen but can be kept to a minimum. (A time management workshop might be the first continuing education event the pastor takes time to attend.)

Finding a place other than one's office in the church may be necessary for uninterrupted study time. This may be a room in your home or a quiet spot in the public library or the library of an educational institution in your community. Having a designated time and place for reading and reflecting can help make certain that these activities take place.

The pastor should be able to negotiate with the congregation for a designated number of days that are to be regarded as continuing education time. Such an agreement allows the pastor to attend a seminar, workshop, pastors' school, or conference for an extended period of time. Some pastors find that a few days or a week in a retreat setting, either alone or with colleagues, for part of the time can also be a means of renewal and learning.

Money

Attending special educational events will require not only time but money. Because religious denominations and congregations have begun to recognize the need for continuing education for clergy, they are also providing funds. Financing of continuing education is happening in various ways. Some congregations are putting into the annual budget of the church a sum designated for continuing education, sometimes not just for the pastor but (in larger congregations) for other staff as well. Sometimes funds are available from the denomination or regional grouping to supplement what the local church provides. From an income tax perspective, it is better for the congregation to pay continuing education fees *for* the minister, than to increase the minister's salary and let the minister pay the full amount.

Scholarship and travel subsidies are sometimes available from the sponsoring organization. Of course, there are opportunities for clergy to attend workshops or seminars in the area in which they live. These may be for one day or less and require little travel. Such events may be sponsored by a hospital, an educational institution, a government agency, or even by a local ministerial association. Often there is no charge or a minimal fee.

A local church can set up an ongoing endowment fund that will generate annual income to be used for continuing education. This type of fund would attract special gifts or could be included in a will. Memorial gifts could be designated for the fund. This fund should not be promoted primarily by the minister, lest the minister be accused of too much self-interest. However, an individual might become enthused about this project and, after getting the approval of pastor and congregation, develop a campaign that would solicit special gifts and bequests. If insufficient funds are generated, at least initially, the amount needed annually could be included as a separate line item in the church budget.

Continuing Education Opportunities

In addition to structured programs for continuing education, the pastor has many opportunities to engage in continuing education while carrying out the responsibilities of parish ministry. Each experience in pastoral work can be a learning event if we are open to that possibility. A visit with a parishioner can provide new information. Ask people questions about what they do for a living. How do they do it? Why do they do it? Do they like doing it? Why or why not? Ask them questions about their faith. Let them ask you questions. Reflect on your discussions and relate the experience to your previous pastoral work.

One of the ways we learn from our experiences is by keeping a record of some of the things that happen and ideas that strike us as important. The events themselves may not be as important as our reflections about those experiences. Taking a few minutes toward the end of the day to jot down some insights based on a reading or interaction with other people can enhance our learning. Thoughts that would otherwise be forgotten are there to be examined and pondered again in the light of new experiences.

Sermon preparation may be the single most important regular continuing education experience of the pastor. Whether done entirely alone or as a follow-up to a group experience, wrestling with the Scripture and searching for truth from all sources is surely educational. Rather than resenting or feeling guilty about the time required, the pastor needs to see this as a legitimate use of time. This is an educational privilege even though it requires hard work. You always learn more than you can possibly put into one sermon.

Another opportunity for continuing education somewhat related to preaching is preparing to teach in a particular situation. To educate others, one must first be educated. While the pastor may not be able to teach a class on a regular basis, the pastor should accept some teaching responsibilities. Natural choices are catechism and adult membership classes as well as short-term courses about the meaning of baptism and Holy Communion, preparation for marriage, or dealing with the death of a loved one.

Opportunities for teaching outside the local church may open up as well. For example, teaching a course on religion at a community college can be a great opportunity to relate to people you might not otherwise meet.

Other forms of service to the community, in addition to teaching, can be opportunities for learning as well. With the permission of your congregation, you may be able to accept a leadership role on a board or committee that is not directly related to your role as a pastor.

While time constraints limit the involvement of a pastor in noncongregational activities, a case can be made for such activity. This is especially true if the activity is benefiting the community in some way. The church served by the pastor benefits from the visibility of the pastor, and the pastor's contacts in the community are broadened.

Service on a board or committee of the denomination can also be a valuable learning experience. We have to be careful because these activities can be seductive, making us feel important and letting us escape from local church duties. A minister has to set priorities and limit involvements outside the local church, lest the congregation resent the time spent.

Of course, you can continue your regular reading and study of books and journals in biblical studies, theology, counseling, and other subject areas related to your pastoral work. Some pastors buy books with good intentions, but never get around to reading them. Look at what you have on your shelves. What is there that you really want to read and that would be helpful to you personally and in your ministry? What is missing (perhaps a specific aspect of ministry, or a title you have heard about that intrigues you)?

Keep yourself informed about new books that would interest you. Various professional journals include book reviews or advertisements from publishers about new books. You can contact the publishers of religious books and ask to be placed on their mailing list to receive their catalog.[1]

Subscribe to religious journals. There are journals published about ministry in general, as well as on specific aspects of ministry such as worship and preaching. Some denominations publish a journal for clergy of their denomination.[2] You can subscribe to such a journal even if you are not a member of that denomination. Journals are easier to read than books, so the pastor can use shorter blocks of time for journal reading.

Most clergy spend a lot of time in the automobile, and usually they are traveling alone. Instead of listening to country western music or an all-news station (that keeps repeating what you have already heard), why not listen to a cassette tape? There are cassette services to which you can subscribe, or you can order cassettes you wish to hear. Tapes are available on a variety of topics and may include lectures by seminary faculty members and sermons by noted preachers. You can sometimes tape a lecture at a conference you attend and listen to it again so maximum learning can take place. Libraries also have tape collections, and you can borrow these tapes, usually without cost.

If you can endure it, you might tape some of the sermons you preach on Sunday and play them back. Listen to how you sound and ask if the delivery of the sermon could be improved. Think about the content and structure of the sermon. How could they be improved?

In addition to books, journals, and tapes you purchase for your study, the library is an obvious resource that comes immediately to mind. Many seminary libraries are open to the public upon proper identification. Although you may not be near a theological seminary, you may be within reasonable proximity to a public or university library. Libraries have interlibrary loan arrangements, so your library might be able to get a book for you that it does not own. Furthermore, libraries are responsive to suggestions about books to be purchased, especially if the book would be of general interest.

In addition to the library, think of other agencies that provide information to the public or to their clients and customers. Often booklets or pamphlets are available from a great range of agencies, institutions, and individuals. Law enforcement officers, physicians, attorneys, bankers, funeral directors, the county agent, the urban planner, or the social welfare director are examples of people who have information available. You can visit with them in person or pick up printed material.

In addition to making use of opportunities like these already mentioned, you can develop a specific plan for your own study, once you have determined a need or interest and have considered available resources. Make the plan as specific as possible, listing resources you will use and a timetable you plan to follow. A two-year plan is usually adequate and helpful. You may want to build in some accountability by sharing your plan with a colleague to whom you will report periodically. Or perhaps you and your colleague will develop a plan that you both will agree to follow, thus establishing mutual accountability.

If you are part of a staff, you are already involved with a group of people meeting regularly. Why not relate to one another on an educational basis? Perhaps a portion of the meeting time could include some form of continuing education, or a separate time can be set for focused learning to take place. Pick a topic, a book, an article, an issue or a problem. Covenant that all must read the material and be prepared to share in discussion. One person can preside and/or make the initial presentation. Rotate leadership. This educational approach to being together will likely change (positively, I believe) the way you relate to one another when conducting the business of the church.

If you are the sole pastor of a congregation, initiate or join an ecumenical group of clergy. Or if there are pastors of your denomination not too far away, get together with them on a regular basis. Some small groups of clergy use the lectionary, meeting weekly to share ideas about worship and preaching that relate to the Scripture. Groups such as these are not only educational but serve as an important support group for participants. Instead of seeing themselves as competitors, participants become a caring community.

Some seminaries may offer programs for self-directed study. If there are no organized programs, individual professors may be willing to suggest books or other resources on a specific topic. Several pastors have sent me audio tapes of their worship services or their sermons asking for an analysis. Since time is limited for faculty members to respond to such requests, they may not be able to provide much personal attention but may at least be willing to send the syllabus of the courses they are teaching that might be of interest to you. The syllabus suggests ideas and a bibliography for self-study.

Short-term Programs

Many seminaries offer short-term workshops and courses, especially during the summer. Some of these are as short as five days, while others may extend to two or three weeks. The advent of doctor of ministry degree programs has increased the number of short-term courses offered. Some seminaries offer these courses during an interterm period such as early December or throughout the month of January. Some summer programs are offered at places other than the seminary campus.

Another possibility is to bring the continuing education program to the clergy, rather than expecting the clergy to come to the workshop or seminar. When the stress of the farm crisis was leading to enormous pressure on the farm families in northeastern Colorado, one of their pastors contacted the seminary from which he had graduated and asked, "What can you do to help us?" As a result of that phone call, a team of trained personnel from the pastoral counseling and medical fields made a series of trips to the area. They met with an ecumenical group of pastors and provided them with the understanding and resources that enabled the pastors to better meet the needs of the people in the communities in which they lived. Funding for the program came from the seminary, the hospital, a group grant from a denominational continuing education fund, and the pastors themselves.

This is an example of a group of pastors identifying a need and then finding the resources to meet that need. Sometimes local resources alone can generate a program of continuing education for clergy. A local ministerial association might work with the funeral directors of the area to offer a one-day workshop on dealing with the funeral and bereavement. Or the clergy could work with the physicians and/or the hospital to put together a seminar on dealing with illness or looking at questions related to medical ethics. Such a seminar could focus on the topic of living wills. Clergy and law enforcement people might collaborate on a workshop on crime and punishment.

Study Leave

Religious bodies and local churches need to recognize the necessity of study leaves for pastors. Study leaves for local church pastors can only happen if the congregation sees the importance of such a leave and is willing to help make such a leave possible. This may mean underwriting some of the cost of securing an interim pastor or pulpit supply. It also means accepting the fact that lay people may need to take more leadership in their congregation. The people will need to adjust to the fact that their regular pastor (who knows everybody and knows just what to do) will not available for a number of weeks or months.

Study leaves can take various forms. Some seminaries welcome pastors-in-residence, who can rent on-campus housing, and attend classes, special lectures, and programs. Sometimes the visiting pastor works on a particular topic of special interest, perhaps using one faculty member who specializes in that area as a consultant. Pastors need not go to a seminary to benefit from a study leave. They can gather materials and work on their own in a place of their choosing. Institutions of higher education other than seminaries can offer learning possibilities of all kinds.

A pastoral exchange is another way continuing education can take place. The exchange may be across the ocean or to a congregation not so far geographically, but quite different from the one the pastor usually serves. Although an overseas exchange may seem more glamorous and provide greater contrast, consider the possibility of an exchange with a pastor who serves a congregation much different from the one you serve. A rural pastor could move into the inner city or a suburb, while the inner city or suburban pastor becomes the pastor of a rural congregation. The logistics might be difficult, but it could be done. Sometimes we need to be somewhere else for a while to fully appreciate the place where we spend most of our time.

Instead of an exchange, a pastor on leave can still spend some time in a congregation where ministry is effectively practiced.[3] By being with a congregation that works well, where exciting things are happening, we can learn a great deal about effective ministry. The time spent on site could be brief or extended, although much more could be learned if the visiting pastor could be there longer than a weekend or a week.

In fact, this concept is similar to the one upon which seminaries base their theological field education program. A student becomes an observer/participant/leader in a congregation on a part-time or full-time basis. The student's placement generally lasts a minimum of nine months and often is extended to a year or more. During this time the student meets weekly with the pastor in a supervisory conference and also meets monthly with a lay committee. The student learns by being on site, seeing and experiencing ministry and then reflecting on the experiences. Why not consider this model a useful way of engaging in continuing education?

In his book, *Competent Ministry,* Mark Rouch gives two examples of pastors on study leave with congregations. In one instance a pastor who was on a six month's leave was employed by another congregation, "not only to observe it but also to test some experimental programs of group work in it."[4] In another instance a couple visited and studied several churches where renewal was taking place. Learning about ministry from colleagues is a practical way to participate in continuing education.

The question of who serves a congregation while the pastor is on a study leave has to be considered. (Of course, in an exchange of pastors, that is not a problem.) But with adequate planning, leadership can be arranged. Retired pastors, seminary students, and maybe even seminary professors are potential interim pastors. The length of time involved would be important, as would be the willingness of the laity to assist the interim pastor as much as possible.

To remain effective a pastor must be involved in continuing education. Each pastor must take the initiative to determine what he or she most needs, to determine goals and a plan of action, and then to follow the plan.

13

Taking Care of Yourself

A retired church leader of great prominence was invited to speak to a group of seminary students about professional ethics for clergy. At the conclusion of his address he invited questions from the audience. One student asked, "If you had the opportunity to do so, is there anything in your ministerial career that you would do differently?" Without hesitation, the minister replied, "Yes, I would spend more time with my family." The minister acknowledged that, judged by almost any standard, his ministry had been highly successful. But for that success he had paid a high price—the breakdown of family relationships, culminating in a painful divorce.

Ministers are expected to spend a lot of time helping others. That is really what the ministry is all about—service to others. The needs are unending. The demands upon a minister's time can be enormous. Matthew's Gospel tells us that the mother of the sons of Zebedee came to Jesus asking that James and John be given places of honor in the future kingdom she believed Jesus would establish. When the other disciples heard this, they were indignant. Jesus then talked to all the disciples about the relationship of greatness and servanthood. Jesus said, "Whoever would be great among you must be your servant, and whoever would be first among you must be your servant (Matt. 20:26-27). True greatness, says Jesus, comes only through service.

Can this emphasis on service, however, lead to the neglect of our own needs, even our own health? That certainly is possible, but I do not believe that is what Jesus intended. Concern for others and concern for self are not mutually exclusive. Self-denial and self-fulfillment are not an either-or proposition. When speaking about love, Jesus admonished us first to love God and then to love our neighbor *as ourself* (Mark 12:30-31). Self-love is assumed as being appropriate and normative.

Ministers, perhaps because they are paid servants of the church, often are likely to feel compelled to make the ministry their number one priority. Only when marriage and family problems develop, or when his or her health deteriorates, does the minister realize what is happening. Then it may be too late to save the marriage or regain good health. The thesis of this chapter is that it is important that as a minister you take good care of yourself.

Your Physical Health

A new United Methodist bishop has been assigned to our area. She is a young woman. (I do not know her age but she seems young to me.) The geographical area served by this bishop is huge—the largest area in the United States served by one United Methodist bishop. The area includes the four states of Colorado, Wyoming, Utah, and Montana.

This woman is going to be very busy. I wondered how she would survive the demanding schedule that will surely develop. Shortly after seeing her installed as bishop, I stopped by the YMCA where I try to swim several times a week. Whom should I meet in the lobby but our bishop, along with a Denver pastor. Both were attired in appropriate garb and with equipment in hand were ready to play a game of racquetball.

I was reassured. Our bishop will survive, and not only survive but excel. She knows the importance of exercise. She knows at least one way to deal with stress.

Each person needs to decide what forms of exercise work best for him or her. Walking is probably the easiest to do and the most widely done. It requires no special equipment, other than a good pair of walking shoes and comfortable clothes appropriate to the weather. Even though walking is easy, most of us are tempted to jump in the car and drive to our destination, even if it is only a few blocks away. Let me strongly urge you to walk whenever you can. It does take a little more time than driving, but you see more. It's a wonderful time to do some reflecting, thinking, meditating. You may even meet some interesting people as you walk. Besides, you are reducing pollution and using less petroleum.

If walking cannot be included in your routine as you fulfill your daily responsibilities, set aside some time each day to walk for the sake of walking, not because you have to get somewhere. Maybe your spouse or child or a neighbor will walk with you. If you get bored, vary the route. If the weather is bad and you live near a shopping mall, you can walk inside. You may want to invest in some indoor exercise equipment, or join a health club or the YMCA.

Other good exercise includes bicycle riding and swimming. Sports of all kinds can provide good exercise. Tennis, racquetball, handball, basketball, volleyball, bowling, and golf can be a lot of fun and provide exercise and interaction with people. Many ministers enjoy golfing. In Colorado, skiing is a popular sport, with lessons and slopes for beginners readily available. Cross-country skiing is gaining in popularity and provides more exercise than downhill skiing. It's less expensive as well. Hiking is a good summer activity to replace the winter sports.

Diet is another important factor in maintaining good health. Someone has said, "You are what you eat." That may be overstating the case, but people are becoming increasingly aware of the importance of good nutrition. If you are not well informed about nutrition, this can be one of your continuing education projects. Because of schedules that can become hectic, it is easy to get into the habit of grabbing junk food to ease those hunger pains. If you know you are overweight or have some bad eating habits, do not wait for the doctor to tell you to change. Take the initiative yourself and change. It can be done.

If you are a smoker, you need to heed the warning on each package of cigarettes. Evidence continues to mount as to the serious consequences of smoking. I once had a parishioner who frequently would wave a $100 bill in my face and say, "If you can get me to quit smoking, you get this $100 bill." I never collected the money because only he could actually quit. It can be done, and there are programs to help you do it.

The use of alcoholic beverages has been a controversial issue in our country and in the life of the church. Some religious denominations require abstinence by its members and its clergy. Other religious groups advocate moderation. All clergy know of the tragedies the abuse of alcohol has directly or indirectly caused. Unfortunately, some clergy have had their ministerial careers ended by the disease of alcoholism. If your use of alcoholic beverages may be a problem for you or others, seek some professional counseling and do not let your career and even your life be ruined.

Getting enough rest is another important component in maintaining physical health. People seem to differ in the amount of sleep necessary for their well-being. For some people, eight hours of sleep are required in order to stay in good health and to be able to function well the next day. Other persons seem to do well with as few as six hours. Some experimentation will help you decide what amount of sleep you need. Once you know what that amount is, try to schedule your time so you get it.

Notice that I said "try." We know that there will be times when you will not get the sleep you need. Emergencies do arise. Your sense of duty may cause you to forego sleep in order to be with an accident victim and that person's family. If you are deprived of sleep because of a pastoral emergency, it certainly should be acceptable for you to get some rest the next day. You need to acknowledge your physical limitations and give yourself permission to rest when you know you need to rest. Too little sleep over an extended period of time can result in a breakdown in health. If you become ill and cannot carry out your pastoral duties, you have paid a high price for thinking you were indefatigable.

Medical and dental examinations on a regular basis should be an essential part of your health plan. Most health insurance companies encourage preventive medicine. Early detection of any medical problem can make a great difference in whether or not the treatment is successful. Waiting until you are seriously ill before seeing a physician is a bad mistake. Likewise, waiting until your teeth are giving you trouble before seeing a dentist is unwise.

Your Emotional Health

The relationship between physical health and emotional health is now widely accepted. If a person is physically ill, there will be an emotional effect as well. Likewise, we know that emotions can profoundly affect our physical health. A physical pain may actually be caused by emotional stress.

Think of the way we speak about pain. If another person makes us angry or frustrated, we may respond by saying, "You give me a pain in the neck." There is more truth in that statement than we realize. Another person's attitude, words, or actions can cause us to feel an actual pain in the neck or in some other part of the body.

Headaches can come from emotional stress. It is not unusual to hear someone say about a difficult or unpleasant task, "This assignment is giving me a headache." And indeed, that may literally be true. Worry can lead to all kinds of physical problems. The word "psychosomatic" is often used to describe this interrelatedness between physical and mental health.

Hardly anyone would deny that the ministry is a stressful vocation. Instead of being employed by one person or having one boss, the minister is employed by an entity made up of many persons. Each of these persons can say, with some degree of accuracy, "the minister works for me. I pay part of the minister's salary." Some persons will take their understanding of this relationship one step further, saying "Therefore, the minister should say and do things that please me." But is that humanly possible? I think it was Abraham Lincoln who said that, "You can please some of the people all the time. You can please all of the people some of the time. But you cannot please all of the people all of the time."

The minister must accept the reality of that statement. At any given time there will be some people in the congregation who will not be entirely pleased with something said or done by the minister. In fact, an action may be taken by the church through one of its decision making bodies, but the minister will be seen as the one ultimately responsible. Or if antagonism develops between two church members, the minister may need to be the mediating influence, to bring about some healing and reconciliation.

Part of the minister's job is to interpret to people the unreasonable expectations that may be placed upon a pastor. Much of what the minister does is invisible to the majority of the congregation. Most people only see the minister on Sunday morning leading worship. They are not aware of the preparation time required for leading worship and preaching. Nor are they really aware of the administrative and pastoral needs that must be met by the pastor. Good communication and reporting by the pastor can increase awareness of what a minister does.

However, regardless of how well the minister communicates, there is no denying that the role of the minister can be stress producing. Not only are there enormous time demands, but any position that involves constant interaction with people can lead to conflict and stress. People are what make the ministry such a gratifying occupation, but people can also be the source of much frustration. Since we know stress cannot be entirely avoided, what we need to consider are some ways of managing stress. Our goal is to maintain good emotional health.

Let me emphasize again the importance of maintaining physical health in order to achieve good emotional health. Proper diet, regular exercise, and sufficient rest are essential. Do you remember the story of Elijah? After Elijah's great triumph at Mt. Carmel, Jezebel vowed to have Elijah killed. Elijah went a day's journey into the wilderness. Sitting under a broom tree, he said he was ready to die. He asked God to take his life, believing that he was the only one left who believed in the true God.

Elijah was in a state of severe depression. He was tired. He was hungry and thirsty. He was lonely. But he prayed to God and a miracle happened. He slept, and during his sleep an angel brought him food and water. After he had rested and received food and water, his attitude changed. He accepted the assignment that God had given him and left the wilderness (1 Kings 19:1-16).

We can learn from the experience of Elijah. Depression may follow some great event, when there is a psychological letdown and the routine of our life returns. Depression can come when we are very tired, hungry, and thirsty, needing the necessities of life. Loneliness, whether of our choosing or a matter of circumstances, can lead to depression. What this suggests is the importance of maintaining good physical health and building positive interpersonal relationships. (The importance of prayer in our lives will be dealt with later.)

A minister needs some hobbies. Especially good hobbies are those that involve physical activity, such as some of the sports mentioned earlier. Gardening is a rewarding activity that provides a useful or pleasing return for the effort. Sometimes in the church not much growth seems to take place, so it's a joy to see something you have planted grow and produce food to be harvested or flowers to admire. Woodworking is another activity that requires working with hands to produce tangible results. Crafts of various kinds, including sewing, pottery, and drawing can provide a meaningful contrast to the other responsibilities of a minister. I even enjoy painting a room; that allows me to see quickly that I've accomplished something .

A minister needs some friends who are not parishioners. This is not to say that ministers and parishioners cannot be friends. However, the role of the pastor sometimes is a barrier to deeper friendship. The pastor cannot share with a parishioner some frustrations because to do so would be to betray confidences. Also, the pastor must be cautious about spending so much time with a few families or persons that other parishioners become resentful. A closer relationship with some persons than with others is inevitable, but a wise pastor will not let it get out of hand.

When I was a parish pastor I found it helpful to have some friends outside of my congregation. Sometimes these were people in other professions whom I got to know and liked. Sometimes these were other clergy, including the Catholic priest who in one community lived only a few houses from my home.

If the pastor is married, friendships with other couples is important. For several years my wife and I were part of a group made up of four ministers and their wives. We called ourselves "The Awful Eight" and met monthly in someone's home for a meal and conversation. Each couple lived in a different community but not a great distance from the others. We were ministers of the same denomination who had known each other (at least slightly) prior to forming the group. Our monthly gatherings were an important factor in keeping all of us emotionally well, I'm sure.

Your Financial Health

Persons who seek ordination as elders in the United Methodist Church are asked a series of questions by the bishop in the presence of the lay and ministerial members of the conference in which they are to be ordained. One question that usually causes some hesitation is: "Are you in debt so as to embarrass you in your work?"[1] Usually a titter of nervous laughter is heard and then each one answers no. Apparently the only reason that people feel they can answer no is because they are not embarrassed by their indebtedness. They are troubled by it and anxious about how it will be paid. But debt is an accepted way of life and almost inevitable for persons who are required to have seven or more years of education beyond high school.

Our seminary, like many other educational institutions, holds an alumni phone-a-thon every year. One of the calls I made recently was to a woman pastor in a small midwestern town. She had graduated less than two years earlier. When asked whether she would like to contribute to the annual fund of the seminary, she said. "I would like to contribute, but I have an indebtedness of about $25,000 from going to school. When that's paid off I will consider contributing to the school."

Some students, like this woman, are graduating from seminary and entering the pastoral ministry with a large debt. Financial compensation for clergy is not so great that this indebtedness will be quickly paid. Careful fiscal management is necessary if these heavily indebted persons are going to succeed in their ministry. In fact, in this day of the ever-handy credit card, all clergy need to practice good fiscal management. But we all know that is easier said than done.

Four aspects of money management require the attention of everyone, including clergy—what we earn, give, spend, save.

1. *What we earn.* Determining the compensation received by a clergy person can be difficult because the compensation is received in various forms. In addition to a cash salary, the minister may be provided with a home or a housing allowance. If the home is owned by the church, no real estate taxes need be paid. Parsonage, utility, and repair costs are usually paid by the church. In addition, the minister is generally reimbursed for church-related travel and other professional expenses. Continuing education funds may be provided, and the premiums for medical insurance and pension benefits may be partially or fully paid by the church. Fees and honoraria for weddings, funerals, and outside speaking engagements may be another source of income for the pastor.

From a tax standpoint, it is advantageous if the compensation received by the pastor is categorized as indicated above. For example, a housing allowance, to the extent actually used, is not included as salary for federal income tax purposes. However, the housing allowance is included as income in the determination of the social security tax.

Churches need to be fair (and generous if possible) in providing a salary package for their clergy. The finance committee and the pastor need to be sure they understand the tax laws regarding compensation for clergy and then structure the package in the way that is most beneficial for the pastor and the church. The pastor needs to appreciate the fact that the tax laws provide some special provisions for clergy and that the compensation includes more than the cash salary.

2. *What we give.* Christianity advocates giving. Christians are called to give of their time, talent, and treasure. One of the reasons Christians give is because "God so loved the world that God gave" (John 3:16). The one whose name we take when we call ourselves "Christian" modeled for us the kind of loving, caring, and giving that we seek to emulate.

Clergy are expected to give in the same way they encourage and invite others to give. The stewardship sermon preached by the minister is preached to the minister, as well as to all others present. Proportionate giving seems to be advocated most often. Thus, the person who receives more is expected to give more. The Hebrew Bible's tithe (ten percent of what one has received) is still a useful standard for giving.

My experience with clergy indicates that they are generous people who practice what they preach. They indeed model a pattern of giving that sets a high standard. Although the congregation they serve is the primary recipient of their giving, clergy give to a wide variety of causes. Educational institutions from which they graduated, local community concerns, and special projects are some of the other beneficiaries of their giving. Sometimes a church looks only at the money given to the church and concludes that a particular donor is not very generous. What they may not realize is how much this individual may be giving to other worthy causes.

People who give generously always seem to have enough left over to meet their other needs. In fact, they speak of the blessing they receive through their giving. Clergy and all who call themselves Christians should give "with glad and generous hearts" (Acts 2:46).

3. *What we spend.* Every day we are bombarded with the message to "buy, buy, buy." Newspapers, magazines, radio and television look to their revenue from advertisers to maintain their existence. Direct mail advertising comes into our homes with almost every mail delivery. Salespeople ring our doorbell to push a product they claim we need.

Not only are we told to buy, but we are also told how easy it is to buy. "No down payment, easy installment plan, cash rebate," are some of the phrases that grab our attention. And what about all those pieces of plastic that we carry in our wallets or purses? "Your credit limit has just been increased" says the insert mailed with your credit card bill.

Is it any wonder that people spend more than they should, and that personal bankruptcy is on the increase? Spending has become too easy with the "buy now, pay later" philosophy that is so widely accepted. Somehow, that piece of plastic makes it seem like you are not spending real money, but later you find out you were.

Clergy and their families can easily get into trouble unless they learn to spend wisely rather than impulsively. "Living within one's means" has to be reintroduced into our thinking if indeed it has been forgotten or never learned. Preparing a budget and then sticking to it may be the best way to avoid financial woes.

The importance of adequate insurance coverage must be stressed. Insurance premiums are not cheap, but they are less expensive than the cost of a major catastrophe. Make certain that your personal property is insured. If you live in a church-owned parsonage, the insurance paid for by the church may only cover the building, not its contents. You may need to take out a separate personal property policy. Some clergy also carry personal liability coverage, so if a malpractice claim is upheld against them, the insurance company will be responsible for payment. Insurance for long-term health care is now available, and the younger we are, the less expensive the premium. This kind of insurance is worth considering.

4. *What we save.* If we succumb to all the advertising, we may have little money to save. To be successful in saving, most persons find it necessary to budget a specified amount that is put aside regularly. Save first and then spend is a good rule to follow.

Many people will gladly give you advice on how to invest the money you save. Be cautious, because some of these advisors will not be objective. They are more interested in selling something that gives them a profit than they are in your financial welfare. Clergy tend to be trusting people and are sometimes taken in by financial scams. Educate yourself in regard to financial matters if this is an area where your knowledge is limited. This could be one of the topics you pursue as part of your continuing education.

Suppose you decide to invest some money monthly in a no-load mutual fund that has a good record. Some funds will accept monthly payments as low as $25.00. If this is a fund that invests in common stocks of major corporations, there will be some fluctuation in the price or value of each share. If you invest the same amount monthly, your money will buy more shares when the price is low and fewer shares when the price is high (cost averaging). If the trend of the mutual fund is upward over a period of several years, you will have made a good investment.

If you can leave your dividends with the mutual fund for reinvestment, you will have the benefit of compounding the value of your investment. Each dividend reinvested adds to the value of your investment upon which the next dividend is paid. If your money is in an Individual Retirement Account (IRA), you pay no taxes on the increase in value of your investment until you withdraw funds for your retirement. Annuities offered by insurance companies offer a similar advantage.

Ministers need to think well ahead about retirement, especially if they expect to live in a church-owned parsonage during their career. Until retirement, the minister and the minister's family live comfortably, but when the minister retires, a home is no longer provided. Now, suddenly, the minister must rent or buy a place to live. Over the years, real estate has tended to increase in value because of inflation and desirability. People who have owned their own home for a long time may find, upon retirement, that their home is valued at three or four times their original purchase price.

Clergy have dealt with this situation in several ways. Some have requested a housing allowance and purchased a home, hoping they will be in the same location long enough for the value of the home to increase substantially. Since in a particular location property values may go down as well as up and the length of a pastorate can be difficult to predict, there is some risk in this plan. However, it may be a risk worth taking.

Other clergy have invested in a home that they rent out until they retire. Then the home can be occupied by the minister or sold if the minister wishes to live somewhere else. A variation on this same idea is to purchase a vacation home, or second home. The pastor and family can enjoy using it and also rent it out for income. At the time of retirement, the property can become the permanent home of the pastor or can be sold and a home purchased in another location. Or the pastor can use the funds from the sale of the home to rent an apartment or home.

If the purchase of real estate is not possible or desirable, the minister needs to be putting some money into investments that will provide funds for housing upon retirement. Certainly the minister should put the maximum possible into her or his pension plan. Unless for reasons of conscience the pastor feels otherwise, the pastor should participate in the social security program.

Your Family

While some Protestant clergy are single, the majority are married. Before we end this chapter, something needs to be said about the relationship of ministers to spouse and to children.

In *The Eternal Triangle*, Robert L. Randall talks about the relationship between pastor, spouse, and congregation. In the preface to the book, he makes it clear that he is not writing only to married clergy. His thesis is that "both a masculine and feminine presence are required by a congregation." If the pastor is an unmarried male, "the congregation will seek out a central feminine presence, perhaps a church secretary, nun, or strong laywoman. When a congregation is headed by a female pastor, it will seek out a central male presence, whether that be her spouse, a strong layman, or a denominational leader."[2] Randall says that his analysis can be applied in any religious group setting, although his insights developed out of his counseling with Protestant clergy and spouses, and in his dealings with Protestant churches in conflict.

Randall talks about the importance of the pastor's having self-awareness and a feeling of well-being. He then explains that all of us have "selfobjects" to whom we relate. He says, "A selfobject is not simply a person we depend upon or whom we love. Selfobjects are those individuals or groups, maybe even those animals or machines, that we make part of us, whose response to us will come as we want it or need it."[3]

All of us need positive relationships with selfobjects to have a sense of well-being. Because the congregation is analogous to an individual self, the congregation has a kind of self-cohesion or corporate personality that interacts with the minister and the spouse. Although congregations are more understanding of the needs of pastor and spouse than they once were, Randall says that "each parish still expects its pastor and related spouse to serve as its mirroring, idealized, or alter ego self objects."[4] When pastor and/or spouse fail to meet these expectations, however unrealistic they may be, the reaction will be negative.

Probably this expectation that the pastor and the pastor's family will be the embodiment of perfection is the most difficult problem the minister will confront. Fortunately this kind of thinking is diminishing, albeit slowly. No longer do churches expect the spouse to be "Mrs. Minister," the unpaid, full-time, assistant pastor. Too many spouses are employed outside the home, pursuing their own careers, for that old viewpoint to prevail. Some ministers now live in their own housing, which may be quite distant from the church. This means the minister's family need not feel they are living in a fishbowl where all their actions are observed and critiqued. Education must continue, but much progress has been made.

The work of the minister is important, but not more important than the minister's family. The minister needs to take time off to be with the family at important times in their lives. It is legitimate to schedule time with your spouse or family. Write it in your personal appointment book and simply say to the committee chairperson who wants to schedule a special meeting, "Sorry, I've got a prior commitment that I cannot break." You might even suggest that the committee could meet without you. It took me several years in the parish ministry before I accepted that fact and convinced the congregation that I did not need to be present at every meeting. That means the pastor gives up some authority, and shares some power. But think of it as a vote of confidence in the laity. It is their church, as well as your church.

14

Renewing Your Faith

People enter the ordained ministry in response to a sense of divine call. Whether this call is experienced dramatically or quietly, the person encounters God in a personal and significant way. Unfortunately, this sense of call can fade. Our feeling of a personal relationship to Christ can weaken. We forget that we must be as intentional about maintaining our spiritual health as we are about maintaining our physical health. If we are to continue to be effective in ministry, our personal spirituality needs to be maintained. Spiritual renewal must be a priority, the "one thing needful" that Jesus urged upon Mary and Martha.

Mary and Martha, along with their brother Lazarus, lived in the little village of Bethany. The two sisters were good friends of Jesus. Apparently their home was a place Jesus could feel comfortable and relaxed. It was probably a favorite stopping place for Jesus when he traveled through that area. Luke's Gospel tells us that on one occasion, Mary engaged Jesus in conversation while Martha rushed into the kitchen to prepare some food for their distinguished guest (Luke 10:38-42). When Mary continued talking with Jesus instead of helping prepare the refreshments, Martha became indignant. She complained to Jesus, "Lord, do you not care that my sister has left me to serve alone? Tell her to help me" (Luke 10:40).

What an awkward position for Jesus! He was being asked to take sides in a little family dispute. Jesus reminded Martha: "Martha, Martha, you are anxious and troubled about many things; one thing is needful. Mary has chosen the good portion, which shall not be taken away from her" (Luke 10:41-42).

According to Luke's Gospel, just prior to this visit to the home of Mary and Martha, Jesus told the parable of the good Samaritan, emphasizing that acting out our faith is of great importance (Luke 10:29-37). Immediately following the account of the conversation of Jesus with Mary and Martha, Luke says that Jesus "was praying in a certain place, and when he ceased, one of his disciples said to him, 'Lord, teach us to pray . . .'" (Luke 11:1). Jesus responds by saying to his disciples the now familiar words that we call the Lord's Prayer.

In this sequence of events we see the necessity of both action and reflection. Followers of Christ need to take time to study and pray, as well as to engage in deeds of loving service. There needs to be a balance, a harmony in our lives. The parable of the good Samaritan reminds us that it is not enough to think or talk about being a good neighbor. We become a good neighbor when we act appropriately in response to human need. The rebuke by Jesus of Martha, who was "distracted by much serving," suggests that sometimes our priority needs to be the renewal of the spiritual depth that must undergird our loving service. Finally, the fact that Jesus took time to pray and taught his disciples to pray suggests that we followers of the Christ must take time in our busy lives to pray.

The Example of Jesus

Prayer permeated the life of Jesus from birth to death. As a small child he was taken to the temple at Jerusalem to be presented to God and blessed by the righteous and devout Simeon (Luke 2:22-35). At the age of twelve he was taken to the temple once again by his parents (Luke 2:41-52). His ministry began with baptism in the river Jordan by John the Baptist (Matt. 3:13-17). Then followed forty days of retreat into the wilderness, where he fasted, prayed, and resisted the temptations of the devil (Matt. 4:1-11). Jesus then began to preach and teach and heal.

Luke's Gospel says that before Jesus chose the Twelve to be his disciples, "he went out into the hills to pray and all night he continued in prayer to God" (Luke 6:12). Jesus prayed in the upper room in Jerusalem at that last supper with his disciples. Later that night, before he was betrayed by Judas, he uttered an agonizing prayer in the Garden of Gethsemane. While his disciples kept falling asleep he prayed, "My father, if it be possible, let this cup pass from me; nevertheless not as I will, but as thou wilt" (Matt. 26:39). Even as he was dying on the cross he prayed "Father, forgive them; for they know not what they do" (Luke 23:34).

Truly Jesus was a man of prayer. His ministry was sustained by prayer, even as he himself was sustained by prayer. How can those of us who claim to be his followers fail to see the importance of prayer in our own lives? We need to believe that more things are wrought by prayer than this world dreams possible.

Ways of Renewing Faith

In a little book called *Self-Renewal,* John W. Gardner says that most of the things that prevent self-renewal "are to be found in the mind rather than in external arrangements."[1] Complacency about the status quo and resistance to change seem to be the chief reasons new ideas have such a difficult time being accepted. Society as a whole tends to be complacent and to resist change, but this is also true for individuals. Clergy are no exception, even though they may deny that.

Perhaps the most important thing that has to change in an individual before spiritual renewal can take place is attitude. First, the individual must believe that she or he *needs* renewal. Second, the individual must *want* spiritual renewal to take place in his or her life. Third, the individual must be willing to *do what is necessary* for renewal to take place.

Most clergy want to deepen their spiritual life. Here are some suggestions about how obstacles can be overcome and the prayer life of the pastor can be sustained

1. *Schedule a regular time.* If you are serious about making prayer a regular part of your daily schedule, you need to plan for it. Exceptions may arise, but they should remain exceptions. We can gain an appreciation for daily prayer and worship from the monastic communities. The liturgy of the hours is an important part of their lives. The monks come together at stated times during the day and evening to share in prayer and worship. In our own way, we need to impose upon ourselves the discipline of regular times for personal and corporate prayer. A time of prayer upon arising in the morning is a good way to begin the day. Perhaps your schedule allows a brief devotional time over the noon hour. And why not end your day with prayer as you reflect on the experiences of the day and recall special needs that weigh on your heart?

2. *Have a special place.* Prayer can take place any time and any place (at least theoretically), but it takes on added meaning if you have a designated place. Perhaps you are the first to arise in the morning and you

can sit at the kitchen table before breakfast. Perhaps you have a study in your home that is your special place, or you may choose your office in the church as your sacred space. Some pastors like to sit in the sanctuary (nave) of the church for their time of meditation and prayer. Weather permitting, an outside spot may be most inspiring. Find a place that is special for you and make it your sacred space.

3. *Find the joy of prayer.* Finding time to pray may seem like a burden. It is one more thing you should do, and you already have so many other things to do. But to see prayer as a burden is to misjudge it. There is an ancient legend that when God first created birds, they had no wings. Later, God gave them wings and the birds immediately complained about the burden being placed upon their body. Then they discovered that these *burdens* were wings that enabled them to fly. So it is with prayer. What we may perceive as a burden is really a gift from God, a means of sending our thoughts heavenward and experiencing the presence of God in our lives. When we think of prayer as something we *must* do, then it becomes an *ought.* James Fenhagen says "a persistent sense of 'ought' has a way of draining us of our creative energies."[2] When our feelings of guilt about not praying as much as we should motivate us to pray, we may pray grudgingly and with resentment. If this is true, then the joy that prayer should bring will not be present. Indeed, as Fenhagen puts it, "At its deepest level, prayer is not something *we do,* but something which the Holy Spirit does *in* and *through us.* To say we 'ought' to pray is like saying we ought to breathe."[3]

The story of Brother Lawrence has always intrigued and inspired me. Brother Lawrence, a humble lay brother in a Carmelite monastery, was cook for the brothers and had many duties. Because of his responsibilities the set times of devotion meant less to him than the habit he developed of referring all he did to God. It took persistence to form this habit, but in the end it became the constant practice of his life. In the midst of the pots and pans, God was his constant friend and companion. With each task he turned to God for help. When he failed he did not just pray for forgiveness, but he confidently expressed his dependence upon God. "It is You who must hinder my falling," he said, "and mend what is amiss." Brother Lawrence wrote, "I cannot imagine how religious persons can live satisfied without the practice of the Presence of God."[4]

In a conference I attended, John Sutherland Bonnell once shared a personal experience to show how prayer can be appropriate and meaningful at any time and in any place. Although he was pastor of a large church in New York City, he disliked the crowded subways and buses of the city that he used to carry out his ministry in the city. He said that the screaming of the wheels on the rails when the subway train rounded a curve and the general noise and confusion grated on his soul like sandpaper. Then one day he happened to notice that his hand, holding the strap in the center of a swaying crowd, was lifted up in the attitude of prayer. The thought came to him, "After all, these men and women are God's children and life is pressing hard on many of them. How can I better employ my time than in praying for them and myself?"

Dr. Bonnell says that from that moment, all dread of the subway journey disappeared. Each time he traveled the subway he prayed for those around him, and he prayed that he might receive the peace of God and carry it to the sick people he would soon be visiting in the hospital. He said that sometimes he came up out of the subway with a mind and heart at peace and a deep inner stillness such as one might find in prayer in some quiet sanctuary. Maybe we too can turn frustration time into prayer time.

4. *Make use of resources.* Usually we need something to help us focus our thoughts and move us into an attitude of meditation and prayer. Many resources are available:

   a. The Bible immediately comes to mind. The lectionary passages can be reflected upon in depth, not only to write your sermon, but also to speak to you in a deeply personal way. The importance of the Bible as a devotional resource can hardly be overemphasized.

   b. Use your hymnal. Many of the hymns are prayer poems set to music. They are rich in theology and move through the seasons of the church year. You need not sing the song to benefit from slowly reading the words and thinking about the message they convey. Try reading the hymn aloud with expression as you reflect on its meaning.

   c. Devotional guides of all kinds are readily available. The *Upper Room Disciplines* is an annual book of daily devotional readings prepared especially for clergy and other religious leaders.[5] Some denominations provide quarterly devotional booklets with daily readings and prayers. Books of various kinds can be used as resources, especially those that pertain to prayer and spirituality.

   d. Do not overlook the Christian classics. These are often older books that have been reprinted in relatively inexpensive paperback editions. They may be a bit more difficult to read because they were written in an earlier age, but they have withstood the test of time. These classics include such books as *The Confessions of St. Augustine, The Imitation of Christ* by Thomas à Kempis, *The Practice of the Presence of God* by Brother Lawrence, *Table Talks* of Martin Luther, *The Journal of John Wesley,* William Law's *A Serious Call to a Devout and Holy Life, The Journal of George Fox,* and *Revelations of Divine Love* by Juliana of Norwich. More recent books include *A Testament of Devotion* by Thomas Kelly and *The Cost of Discipleship* by Dietrich Bonhoeffer.

5. *Keep a journal.* The value of keeping a journal outweighs the extra effort that is required. Jot down prayer concerns, quotations, insights from your reading and from other experiences. As James Fenhagen puts it in one of his books, "A journal can help us get a feel for the movement of our life as it unfolds in response to the inner prompting of the Holy Spirit. It helps deepen our awareness of where we have been, where we are now and where we seem to be going."[6] Our journal can be as simple or complex as we want or need to make it.

6. *Relate to a spiritual guide.* While men preparing for the priesthood in Roman Catholic seminaries have long been required to have a spiritual guide, the idea of a spiritual guide is something new for many Protestants. It is really quite a simple concept. One person becomes a companion to another person on that person's spiritual journey. The two persons may meet as often as they choose. Some people even serve as a spiritual guide on a long-distance basis, using correspondence and/or the telephone to keep in touch.

The word "mentor" suggests something of what a spiritual guide does. One of the main things is giving support to another person. It is not easy to live a disciplined spiritual life, and the spiritual guide provides encouragement and support, as well as accountability.

Fenhagen suggests five areas he explores with the other person (the companion) when serving as a spiritual guide:

a. the relationship between my companion and myself
b. the ministry to which my companion is committed
c. the discipline he or she has chosen to follow
d. the process of the journey itself
e. the resources that might possibly be helpful.[7]

7. *Join a covenant group.* It is difficult to maintain spiritual health without the support of others. A spiritual guide can be of tremendous

help on a one-on-one basis. However, being included in a small face-to-face group of persons who covenant to help each other grow spiritually is a rewarding experience. The pastor may find such a group within the congregation he or she serves. It may be better, however, if the pastor participates in a group composed of other clergy. As indicated earlier in the book, such a group may be formed to study the lectionary passages and help one another with sermon preparation. Such a group often develops into a strong support community.

8. *Attend a retreat.* A retreat of several days provides time for simply being in God's presence or for concentrated attention on our relationship with God. One of the most memorable experiences in my life was sharing in a silent retreat. The retreat was silent except for some guidance given verbally by the retreat leader and some sharing as the retreat concluded. At first I wondered how I would use the blocks of silence, but I soon developed an appreciation for the privilege of being alone with my thoughts. I learned the difference between the pain of loneliness and the joy of solitude. I found my senses heightened as I saw beauty and design that I would otherwise have overlooked. I heard the sounds of birds and of nature as I walked through the grounds of the retreat center. These were sounds I would have missed if I were conversing with another person.

Some pastors arrange an individual retreat, perhaps to a Roman Catholic monastery for a few days or to some other place of quiet, peace, and privacy. At other times a retreat may bring a group of people together who study, pray, and play in a supportive community. Retreats can bring renewal of mind, body, and spirit.

9. *Pray as you prepare and lead worship.* The pastor, of all people, surely recognizes the importance of corporate worship. James Fenhagen reminds us that one of the ways our spiritual journey is sustained is "regular participation in the corporate worship of the community of faith."[8] However, the very fact that the pastor is the one primarily responsible for planning and leading worship may create a problem. As one pastor admitted to me, "I'm so busy helping others to worship that I feel sometimes that I myself am not really worshipping." This can be a problem but not an insurmountable one.

When preparing the worship service the pastor can actually worship. The entire service, including the sermon, should be prepared in a prayerful way. As you prepare, think of the people who will be singing, praying, and listening when the service takes place. Think of how the words you are thinking, reading, and writing speak to you now, and how they will speak later to the congregation. Then prepare for the service so thoroughly that when it happens you are a full participant, as well as its leader.

When we lead others in worship, we too worship. When we preach, we preach to ourselves as well as to others. Maybe you assume this is the case, but most of us must be intentional about offering our worship and preaching to ourselves if it is to happen. One pastor prays each day in the sanctuary of the church he serves, moving each time to a different pew and remembering in prayer the people who will be sitting in that place come Sunday. Another pastor uses the membership list of the congregation as her prayer list, moving through the list as she prays for specific persons each day.

Teaching Others to Pray

Earlier we noted that the disciples asked Jesus, "Lord, teach us to pray." They had seen and heard Jesus pray. They knew their own prayer life was weak, and they wanted to strengthen it. Many people in our congregations could use some help learning how to pray. They may not ask for such help in a direct way, but deep inside they know this is a lack in their lives. They misunderstand what prayer really is, and they do not know how to pray.

Too many people think of prayer only as asking God for something. An old Russian proverb says that what people often ask for when they pray is that two and two will not equal four. Our prayers of asking (our prayers of petition) often reveal a misunderstanding of prayer. Prayer is not a blank check with God's signature on the bottom. It is not like a parachute to be saved for emergency use only, or like a child's letter to Santa Claus, begging for certain things. Yet these ideas are evident in the way people pray. Too often our prayers are self-centered instead of God centered.

Prayer is much more than asking, although asking is a part of prayer. As Harry Emerson Fosdick once said, "Petition is only one province in the vast Kingdom of prayer."[9] It is not the whole kingdom, just one province. Prayer is communion with God, fellowship with the most high. Prayer is opening our lives to God so God's will can be done in us and through us. Prayer is experiencing the love of God in such a way that we are motivated to reach out in love to others.

Pastors need to offer instruction in prayer. Many resources are available. The workbooks on prayer written by Maxie Dunnam can be used in a group or by individuals.[10] In many churches, the midweek prayer meeting for the whole congregation is a thing of the past, but small fellowship or undershepherd groups can be formed in a church. These small covenant groups can make devotional Bible reading and prayer an important component of their time together.

John Wesley organized small fellowship groups called classes that really were a key ingredient in the birth and growth of the Methodist church. Class meetings were held in homes, and people studied the Bible, prayed and shared their testimonies. The Christian base communities that have sprung up in recent years in Latin America are somewhat similar. The United Methodist Church in this country is looking to the early Methodist class meeting as a model for the church of today.[11]

A pastor who is willing and able to serve as a spiritual guide to the congregation he or she serves will find an appreciative response. The pastor can help families develop a simple plan for family worship in the home. A special season of the year such as Advent or Lent can be a time to introduce this program to the congregation. Special devotional booklets for these seasons are available from many church publishers, or some congregations invite their own members to contribute the daily meditations.

The pastor can introduce the concept of journal writing as a spiritual discipline. Persons can be trained as undershepherds or as spiritual guides, to work with groups or individuals. People can be guided in praying for specific concerns or persons. One congregation uses its church newsletter to list a person or family to be the focus of the prayers of the people for one week. Also, the newsletter identifies another congregation in the area to be remembered in prayer for a designated period of time. Lay liturgists can be trained to prepare and lead prayers for worship. Some congregations have a telephone prayer chain, so that when a special need develops a series of phone calls will result in a number of people praying on behalf of that special concern.

The goal of the pastor should be to develop a praying church, and that can only happen if the church has a praying pastor who will also teach others to pray.

The book title *Celebration of Discipline* seems to be a contradiction. How can one joyfully celebrate a discipline? In the last chapter of this book, Richard J. Foster explains how this is possible. He notes that joy is one of the gifts of the Spirit (Gal. 5:22) and suggests that people cannot continue very long in any activity without some sense of joy in what they are doing. Furthermore, "in the spiritual life only one thing will produce genuine joy and that is obedience." Expanding upon that idea, Foster says that "Joy comes through obedience to Christ and joy results from obedience to Christ. Without obedience joy is hollow and artificial."[12]

We who serve Christ should find joy in our obedient service, just as we find joy in the practice of prayer. Paul's advice to the Thessalonians is good advice for us today: "Rejoice always, pray constantly, give thanks in all circumstances; for this is the will of God in Christ Jesus for you" (1 Thess. 5:16-18).

Notes

Chapter 1: The Minister as a Caring Person

1. The report of the Readiness for Ministry project is available in two volumes under the title *Readiness for Ministry.* Volume 1, which deals with criteria, was published in 1975. Volume 2 provides an assessment of the project and was published in 1976. The publisher is the Association of Theological Schools in the United States and Canada.

   A pretest questionnaire was completed by more than two thousand persons, and a revised questionnaire was submitted to more than five thousand persons. This continentwide survey resulted in 4,895 usable answer sheets. The respondents included 432 professors in theological schools, 406 senior seminary students, 1,933 seminary alumni who were in active ministry, 318 denominational officials, and 1,806 randomly selected lay persons representing forty-seven denominations. Out of the mass of data that was gathered, the researchers identified sixty-four core clusters of responses. These core clusters were then ranked in order of importance.

2. Paul E. Johnson, *The Psychology of Pastoral Care* (Nashville: Abingdon Press, 1953), 19.

3. Ibid., 21–22.

Chapter 2: Communicating

1. "Competence in the Parish Ministry," The Academy of Parish Clergy, April 22, 1971, revised in 1974.

2. Merrill R. Abbey, *Communication in Pulpit and Parish* (Philadelphia: Westminster Press, 1973), 28, citing Claude E. Shannon, *The Mathematical Theory of Communication;* and Warren Weaver, *Recent Contributions to the Mathematical Theory of Communication* (Champaign: University of Illinois Press, 1949).

3. Abbey, *Communication in Pulpit and Parish,* 31. The model is based on one by David K. Berlo, *The Process of Communication: An introduction to Theory and Practice* (New York: Holt, Rinehart & Winston, Inc., 1960), 72.

4. A news article about the acceptance of a voiceprint in a court case appeared in the *Chicago Daily News* on April 12, 1966. The inventor of the voiceprint was Lawrence G. Kersta, who appeared in court in Westchester County Court in New York to demonstrate the voiceprint. The article states,

"Kersta, a former employee of Bell Telephone Laboratories, developed an electronic method of converting the voice into weird-looking picture displays known as spectographs."

5. Newsletter of the Institute for Advanced Pastoral Studies, November 1965.

Chapter 3: Leading and Supervising

1. H. Richard Niebuhr, *The Purpose of the Church and Its Ministry* (New York: Harper & Row, 1956), 31.
2. *Frequently Noted Characteristics of Effective Pastors.* Unpublished report by Dr. Alan Sager, Trinity Lutheran Seminary, Columbus, Ohio.
3. Ibid.
4. Ibid.
5. R. Robert Cueni, *The Vital Church Leader* (Nashville: Abingdon Press, 1991), 15.
6. Ibid.
7. Ibid.
8. Richard Bondi, *Leading God's People: Ethics for the Practice of Ministry* (Nashville: Abingdon Press, 1989), 64.
9. Cueni, *The Vital Church Leader,* 40.
10. Paul Wilkes, "The Hands That Would Shape Our Souls," *The Atlantic,* Vol 266, December 1990, 59–62.
11. Ibid.
12. Ibid.
13. Donald F. Beisswenger, "Differing Modes of Supervision in Theological Field Education," *Theological Education* (Autumn 1974): 58.
14. This is a modification of a listing by Kenneth Pohly of United Theological Seminary in Dayton, Ohio, and appeared in an unpublished, undated paper entitled "Seminary Models of Supervision: A Review." Pohly drew upon material in Beisswenger's article, mentioned in the preceding footnote.
15. John Classen made the statement in a paper entitled "Process of Supervision," which was presented at the meeting of Canadian Theological Field Educators in Toronto, January 8, 1980. At that time Dr. Classen was Director of Field Education, Queen's Theological College, Kingston, Ontario.
16. Some of the ideas about evaluation expressed in this chapter first came to my attention in an unpublished, undated paper by Ralph W. Spencer entitled "Evaluation in the Context of Field Education," Centre for Christian Studies, Toronto, Canada.
17. I was told that this checklist was first used by a United Methodist bishop and the superintendent ministers who formed the bishop's cabinet. However, I do not know if this is true and thus cannot give credit to any person or group.

Chapter 4: Planning

1. This diagram is my modification of a diagram that appears in *Developing Leaders, Building Communities: A Rural Resource Guide.* The guide was brought to my attention by Michael Dash of the Interdenominational Theological Center in Atlanta. The guide was prepared in 1992 as part of the Rural Communities Project, by the Kellogg Foundation.

2. These criteria for evaluating goals are fairly common, but I first learned of them in the May 1975 *Interpreter,* the program journal of the United Methodist Church, 15–16.
3. Charles Reimnitz, "How Clergymen Use (Misuse) Their Time," *Church Management; The Clergy Journal* (March 1975): 14–16.
4. Ibid.

Chapter 5: Reflecting

1. Jackson W. Carroll, *Ministry as Reflective Practice: A New Look at the Professional Model* (Washington, D.C.: The Alban Institute, 1986), 1–2.
2. Evelyn and James Whitehead, *Method in Ministry,* (New York: Seabury Press, 1981), 2.
3. Ibid.
4. Ibid., 23.
5. Ibid., 22.
6. Ibid., 24.
7. Kenneth Pohly and Luke Smith, "The Use of Narrative in Identity Formation: Implications for Supervision," *Theological Field Education Key Resources,* vol. 5, eds. Don Beisswenger, Doran McCarty, and Lynn Rhodes. (Association for Theological Field Education, 1986), 128–46.
8. William Nelson, "A Narrative Approach to Theological Reflection," *Journal of Supervision and Training in Ministry,* vol. 9 (1987): 157–82.
9. Pohly and Smith, "The Use of Narrative in Identity Formation," 141.
10. Nelson, "A Narrative Approach to Theological Reflection," 158.
11. Ibid., 161. The quotation is from the book by Stanley Hauerwas, with Richard Bondi and David P. Burrell, entitled *Truthfulness and Tragedy: Further Investigation in Christian Ethics* (London: University of Notre Dame Press, 1977), 35.
12. "An Introduction to Theological Reflection," used at the Bairnwick School of Theology, University of the South, Sewanee, Tenn. An expanded explanation of this model appeared in "Everyday Theology: A Model for Religious and Theological Education," *Chicago Studies* 22, no. 2 (August 1983).
13. From "An Introduction to Theological Reflection," 5.
14. Ibid., 1.

Chapter 6: Administration

1. Alvin J. Lindgren, *Foundations For Purposeful Church Administration* (Nashville: Abingdon Press, 1965) 38.
2. Ibid., 60.
3. Ibid., 61–62.
4. Peter F. Rudge, *Ministry and Management: The Study of Ecclesiastical Administration* (London: Tavistock Publications, 1968), 23.
5. H. Richard Niebuhr, *The Purpose of the Church and Its Ministry* (New York, Harper & Brothers, 1956), 31.
6. Alvin Lindgren and Norman Shawchuck, *Management for Your Church: How to Realize Your Church's Potential Through a Systems Approach* (Nashville: Abingdon Press, 1977). When explaining a systems theory of organization, Lindgren and Shawchuck give this definition: "An organizational system is a

set of components that work together to accomplish an overall objective, and that possess a sufficient boundary to distinguish it from its environment" (32). They list six components of an organizational system:

1. The *input system* refers to the raw materials that the church takes in from its environment, such as new people, hired personnel, money, new technologies and methods, materials, and so on.

2. The *transforming system* of a church refers to the means by which the church transforms raw materials into the church's desired results. This process includes three factors that have a dynamic relationship to one another: a. Theological-missional purposes, b. Organizational structures, c. Intra- and interpersonal relationships.

3. The *output system* of a church "is composed of the means by which it exports a part of its resources (money, people, programs, and such) in order to influence its environment or to support other organizations or causes"(37).

4. The *environment* of a system comprises "all other systems (organizational, social, economic, etc.) that seek to influence it, or that the system is seeking to influence"(38). It needs to be added that systems theory suggests that if there is a change in the environment, there most likely needs to be an adaptive change by the system. (For example, if the elderly people living in the neighborhood of the church are moving and selling their homes to young families, the church will need to change its program emphasis.)

5. The *boundary* is the means by which the church, existing within an environment of other systems, is distinguished from these other systems. Boundary "can best be understood in terms of those characteristics of the system which influence or monitor the transactions and exchanges of the church with its environment"(40).

6. Through the *feedback loop* the church can constantly gather information about the effects of its programs and use it to evaluate its performance in relation to its mission purpose statement and its goals. The church cannot expect to be 100 percent successful in its programs, and its environment is constantly changing, even while the church is carrying out its ministries; thus there is a gap between the church's desired outputs and its actual outputs.

7. Alvin Lindgren and Norman Shawchuck, *Management for Your Church*, 140.

8. Marlene Wilson lives in Boulder, Colorado, and conducts seminars and workshops on volunteers. She recently led a seminar for students at Iliff School of Theology at which time she provided this information. She is the author of several books, including *How to Mobilize Church Volunteers* (Minneapolis: Augsburg, 1983).

9. Ibid.

10. Don S. Browning, *A Fundamental Practical Theology* (Minneapolis: Fortress Press, 1991), 279.

Chapter 7: Pastoral Care

1. Larry K. Graham, *Care of Persons, Care of Worlds* (Nashville: Abingdon, 1992), 20.
2. Edmund Holt Linn, *Preaching as Counseling: The Unique Method of Harry Emerson Fosdick* (Valley Forge, Penn.: Judson Press, 1966). See especially pages 14–26. A more recent book, which makes note of Linn's book, also discusses the relationship of pastoral counseling to preaching. See also Donald Capps, *Pastoral Counseling and Preaching* (Philadelphia: Westminster, 1980). Capps sees structural similarities between the sermon and the counseling session.
3. Joseph E. McCabe, *The Power of God in a Parish Program* (Philadelphia: Westminster Press, 1959), 31–38. McCabe has a short chapter entitled "The Counseling Shelf." He also describes the program of pastoral visitation he implemented in his parish.

Chapter 8: Worship

1. Søren Kierkegaard, *Purity of Heart Is to Will One Thing*, trans. Douglas V. Steere (New York: Harper and Row, 1956), 179–81.
2. Evelyn Underhill, *Worship* (New York: Harper & Row, 1957), 3.
3. H. Grady Hardin, Joseph D. Quillian, and James F. White. *The Celebration of the Gospel* (Nashville: Abingdon, 1964), 16. Their exact definition says, "Christian Worship is celebration that relates us to God and to one another, renewing in us the meaning and power of God's victory in Jesus Christ."
4. James F. White, *Introduction to Christian Worship* (rev. ed.) (Nashville: Abingdon Press, 1990), 31.
5. This definition appears in an unpublished one-page list entitled "Some Do's and Don'ts in Writing the Building Program for Worship." At the time Dr. Ritenour was head of the department of church architecture with the National Council of Churches.
6. White, *Introduction to Christian Worship,* 31.
7. Some of these ideas appeared in an article I wrote for *Newsnotes,* published by the Fellowship of United Methodists in Worship, Music, and Other Arts, November 1986. The publication is now named *Worship and the Arts.*
8. *Hallelujah!* No. 2. Section on Worship. General Board of Discipleship, The United Methodist Church, P.O. Box 840, Nashville, TN 37202.
9. In regard to inclusive language, a good resource is a booklet entitled "Words that Hurt, Words that Heal," prepared by the Task Force on Language Guidelines of the United Methodist Church. It is available from Graded Press, The United Methodist Publishing House, P.O. Box 801, Nashville, TN 37202.
10. Grady Hardin, *The Leadership of Worship* (Nashville: Abingdon Press, 1980), 97.

Chapter 9: Preaching

1. A letter dated February 18, 1986, addressed to "Dear Friends of Theological Education at Iliff" was received by the president of the seminary. The letter was by thirty United Methodist clergy, including bishops and district superintendents of the four states of Minnesota, North Dakota, South Dakota,

and Wisconsin. After expressing appreciation for the dedicated effort of the seminary to prepare students for ministry, the letter noted that congregations continually make requests regarding qualifications they wish to have in a pastor. As a result of hearing these requests, these clergy leaders listed three aspects of ministry that they considered "beneficial to effective ministry." The letter was signed by James H. Schneider on behalf of all the clergy who were present at this gathering.

2. This lecture was printed in *Aware*, Spring/Summer 1984, published by Garrett-Evangelical Theological Seminary, Evanston, Illinois. At that time, Dr. Campbell (who had been the pastor of Riverside Church in New York City) was professor of preaching and worship at Garrett-Evangelical Seminary.

3. Sidney Parnes, Ruth Noller, and Angelo Biondi, *Guide to Creative Action* (New York: Charles Scribner's Sons, 1977).

4. Marilee Zdenek, *The Right Brain Experience* (New York: McGraw Hill, 1983), 12.

5. Ibid., 55.

6. Rollo May, *The Courage to Create* (New York: W. W. Norton and Company, 1975), 44.

7. Ibid., 44–45.

8. C. H. Dodd, *The Apostolic Preaching and its Developments* (New York: Harper and Row, 1964), 7–8.

9. Harry Emerson Fosdick, "What's the Matter with Preaching?" *Harper's Magazine* (July 1928), 1–8.

10. Bruce C. Salmon, *Storytelling in Preaching.* (Nashville: Broadman Press, 1988), 25.

11. The use of personal story in preaching is dealt with in a helpful way in Richard L. Thulin, *The "I" of the Sermon* (Fortress Press, 1989). See also my article, "Preaching and Story," *Iliff Review* (Fall 1980): 53–61.

12. This is my modification of a sermon preparation process which was shared with me many years ago by Dr. Herbert J. Doran, who at that time was professor of preaching at Dubuque Theological Seminary in Iowa.

13. For a good review of sermon outlining principles and procedures, see chapters 5 and 6 of Ilion T. Jones, *Principles and Practice of Preaching* (Nashville: Abingdon Press, 1956), 87–123.

14. Michael Rogness, "The Eyes and Ears of the Congregation," *Academy Accents: the Newsletter of the Academy of Preachers* 8, no. 1 (Spring 1992). Dr. Rogness is associate professor of pastoral theology and homiletics at Luther Theological Seminary in St. Paul, Minnesota.

Chapter 10: Christian Education

1. This document was prepared by the Vocation Agency of the United Presbyterian Church in the U.S.A. (1975). The other seven roles of the pastor, according to this document, are: director of worship, faciliator of pastoral care, leader and interpreter of mission, facilitator of parish/community relationships, administrator, member of the presbytery, and member of the profession.

2. Quoted in "The Nature and Mission of the Church," A pamphlet of the Division of Ordained Ministry, The United Methodist Church, 1985.

Chapter 11: Evangelism

1. Patrick R. Keifert, *Welcoming the Stranger: A Public Theology of Worship and Evangelism* (Minneapolis: Fortress Press, 1992), 3.

2. This definition is stated in a folder of the Foundation for Evangelism, 1910 Adelicia Street, Suite 206, Nashville, TN 37212. No date is given on the folder. The foundation was organized in 1949 by Harry Denman and others "committed to keeping evangelism central to Methodism."

3. Richard Stoll Armstrong, *The Pastoral Evangelist in the Parish* (Louisville: Westminster/John Knox Press, 1990), 13.

4. Ibid.

5. George Barna is president of Barna Research Group Ltd., a marketing research company located in Glendale, California. He was interviewed by Cynthia B. Astle for the *United Methodist Reporter*. The summary of the interview appeared in the January 1, 1993, *Reporter*.

6. Tex Sample, *U.S. Lifestyles and Mainline Churches* (Louisville: Westminster/John Knox, 1990), 15.

7. Ibid., 15. Sample cites Daniel Yankelovich, *New Rules: Searching for Self-Fulfillment in a World Turned Upside Down* (New York: Random House, 1981), 111–14.

8. Ibid., 16.

9. Ibid., 17.

10. Ibid., 19.

11. Richard N. Ostling, "Church Search," *Time* (April 5, 1993): 44–49. Roof's findings are discussed in detail in his book *A Generation of Seekers* (New York: Harper and Row, 1993).

12. Ibid., 46.

13. This information appeared in the *Denver Post,* January 31, 1986. The article was provided by the Religious News Service.

14. William Easum, *How to Reach Baby Boomers* (Nashville: Abingdon Press, 1991), 20. The author is the senior minister of Colonial Hills United Methodist Church in San Antonio, Texas.

15. Ibid., 21.

16. Ibid., 21–22.

17. Donald A. McGavran, *Understanding Church Growth,* 3rd ed. rev. and ed. C. Peter Wagner (Grand Rapids: William B. Eerdmans Publishing Co., 1990), xi.

18. Ibid., xiv.

19. George E. Sweazey, *Effective Evangelism* (New York: Harper & Row, 1953), 13.

20. Herb Miller, *How to Build the Magnetic Church* (Nashville: Abingdon Press, 1987), 32. Herb Miller is the executive director of the National Evangelistic Association of the Christian Church (Disciples of Christ).

21. Ibid.

22. The results of this research are given in the *Action/Information Newsletter* (September 1977), The Alban Institute, Mount St. Alban, Washington, D.C. 20016.

23. The results of the Gallup poll were printed in the *Denver Post,* July 23, 1988. The information was based on 2,556 interviews conducted between March 11 and March 20, 1988.

Chapter 12: Continuing Your Education

1. For example, Augsburg Fortress publishes *Book Newsletter*, which includes not only reviews of books they have published but reviews of books from other publishers as well. To request *Book Newsletter*, write to Augsburg Fortress Publishers, Box 1209, Minneapolis, MN 55440.
2. The one I receive regularly is the *Circuit Rider*, published primarily for United Methodist clergy. A sample copy can be secured by writing *The Circuit Rider*, P.O. Box 801, Nashville, TN 37202.
3. Mark Rouch mentions this possibility in *Competent Ministry: A Guide to Effective Continuing Education* (Nashville: Abingdon Press, 1974), 91.
4. Ibid.

Chapter 13: Taking Care of Yourself

1. *The Book of Discipline of the United Methodist Church* (Nashville: The United Methodist Publishing House, 1988), 426.
2. Robert L. Randall, *The Eternal Triangle* (Minneapolis: Fortress Press, 1992), vii.
3. Ibid., 19.
4. Ibid.

Chapter 14: Renewing Your Faith

1. John W. Gardner, *Self Renewal* (New York: Harper and Row, 1964), 43.
2. James C. Fenhagen, *More Than Wanderers: Spiritual Disciplines for Christian Ministry* (New York: Seabury Press, 1978), 29.
3. Ibid.
4. Brother Lawrence, *The Practice of the Presence of God* (Nashville: The Upper Room Publishing Co., 1950), 32.
5. *The Upper Room Disciplines* annual book can be ordered from The Upper Room, 1908 Grand Avenue, Nashville, TN 37203.
6. James C. Fenhagen, *More Than Wanderers*, 62.
7. Ibid., 77.
8. James C. Fenhagen, *Mutual Ministry* (New York: Seabury Press, 1977), 84.
9. Harry Emerson Fosdick, *The Meaning of Prayer* (Glasgow, Scotland: William Collins Sons & Co. Ltd, 1960), 145. The book was first published in 1915 in Great Britain.
10. The first of these was entitled *The Workbook of Living Prayer* followed by *The Workbook of Intercessory Prayer*. These and other devotional resources are available from The Upper Room, 1908 Grand Avenue, P.O. Box 189, Nashville, TN 37202.
11. For information on "Covenant Discipleship: The Early Methodist Class Meeting for the Church of Today," write to Covenant Discipleship, P.O. Box 840, Nashville, TN 37202.
12. Richard J. Foster, *Celebration of Discipline* (New York: Harper and Row, 1978), 164–65.

Index

Scripture Index

Subject/Author Index